T0340579

CfE Third Level
MATHS
PRACTICE QUESTION BOOK

Craig Lowther • Ian MacAndie

CfE Third Level MATHS
PRACTICE QUESTION BOOK

001/22032018

10 9 8 7 6 5 4 3 2 1

ISBN 9780008263546

Published by

Leckie & Leckie Ltd

An imprint of HarperCollinsPublishers

Westerhill Road, Bishopbriggs, Glasgow, G64 2QT

T: 0844 576 8126   F: 0844 576 8131

leckieandleckie@harpercollins.co.uk   www.leckieandleckie.co.uk

Special thanks to

Jouve (layout and illustration); Ink Tank (cover design);
Project One Publishing Solutions (project management);
Jess White (editing); Nick Hamar (answers)

A CIP Catalogue record for this book is available from the
British Library.

Acknowledgements

Whilst every effort has been made to trace the copyright holders,
in cases where this has been unsuccessful, or if any have
inadvertently been overlooked, the Publishers would gladly
receive any information enabling them to rectify any error or
omission at the first opportunity.

Printed in Italy by Grafica Veneta S.P.A

How to use this book iv

UNIT 1   NUMBER, MONEY AND MEASURE

UNIT 2   SHAPE, POSITION AND MOVEMENT

UNIT 3   INFORMATION HANDLING

ANSWERS
www.leckieandleckie.co.uk/page/Resources

How to use this book

Welcome to Leckie and Leckie's *CfE Third Level Maths Practice Question Book*. This book follows the structure of the Leckie and Leckie *CfE Third Level Maths Student Book*, so is ideal to use alongside it. Questions have been written to provide practice for topics and concepts which have been identified as challenging for many students.

Examples

Examples with worked solutions provide support for particularly tricky concepts.

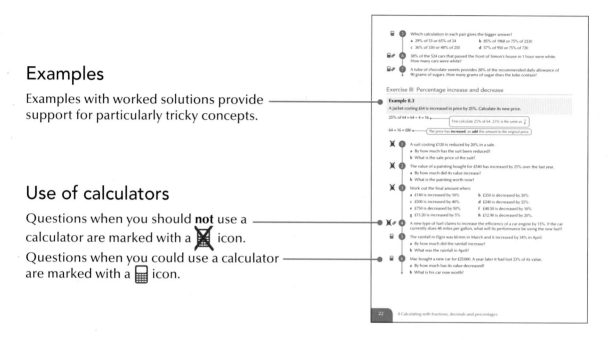

Use of calculators

Questions when you should **not** use a calculator are marked with a ✗ icon.

Questions when you could use a calculator are marked with a ▦ icon.

Reasoning questions

Questions which require reasoning skills are marked with a ⚙ icon.

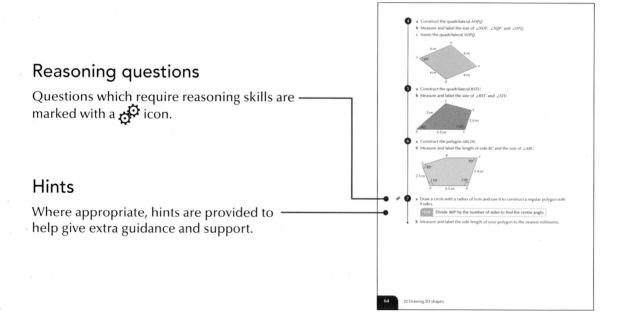

Hints

Where appropriate, hints are provided to help give extra guidance and support.

Answers

Check your own work. The answers are provided online at:

www.leckieandleckie.co.uk/page/Resources

1 Estimation and rounding

Exercise 1A Rounding

1. Round each of these numbers to the nearest:
   i 10   ii 100   iii 1000
   a 6248   b 7476   c 2539   d 1968
   e 762   f 247   g 499   h 34752
   i 18536   j 80909   k 8080   l 1999

2. Round each of these numbers to:
   i the nearest whole number   ii 1 decimal place.
   a 6.28   b 1.54   c 9.04   d 5.59
   e 3.823   f 9.449   g 5.465   h 12.56
   i 156.92   j 86.45   k 10.08   l 6.455

3. Round each of these numbers to:
   i 2 decimal places   ii 3 decimal places.
   a 1.6244   b 6.7258   c 8.4546   d 4.6773
   e 37.04384   f 752.64265   g 10.916843   h 61.007282
   i 8.0599873   j 54.286286   k 3.46772745   l 48.99999999

Exercise 1B Estimates to calculations

Example 1.1

Estimate the answers to these calculations.

a 54×37 b $477 \div 82$

a $54 \times 37 \approx 50 \times 40$ Round each number to the nearest 10.
$= 2000$

b $477 \div 82 \approx 480 \div 80$
$= 6$

1. Estimate the answers to these calculations by rounding each number to the nearest 10.
   a 13×22 b 61×34 c 42×78 d 58×81 e 92×29
   f 88×57 g 75×48 h 66×97 i 82×86 j 96×97

2. Estimate the answers to these calculations by rounding the larger number to the nearest 100 and the smaller one to the nearest 10.
   a $2103 \div 71$ b $1523 \div 48$ c $479 \div 52$ d $1792 \div 62$ e $828 \div 39$
   f $1373 \div 68$ g $1181 \div 28$ h $4212 \div 55$ i $581 \div 63$ j $1609 \div 77$

3. Estimate the answers to these calculations by rounding each number to the nearest 10.
   a $\dfrac{354 + 52}{182 + 23}$ b $\dfrac{247 + 96}{28 + 44}$ c $\dfrac{164 + 118}{68 - 32}$

   d $\dfrac{328 - 59}{18 + 14}$ e $\dfrac{166 + 148}{58 + 19}$ f $\dfrac{538 - 63}{84 - 19}$

4 Estimate the answers to these calculations by rounding the larger number to the nearest 10 and the smaller number to 1 decimal place.

a 28×0.34 b 42×0.81 c 73×0.44 d 94×0.54

e 86×0.33 f 153×0.25 g 213×0.42 h 623×0.54

5 Estimate the answers to each of these calculations.

a $3452 - 198$ b $1383 + 682$ c 678×23 d $715 \div 83$

e 613×592 f $136.4 \div 68.5$ g $\dfrac{81.4 + 78.8}{98.3 - 19.9}$ h $\dfrac{828 + 67.6}{16.9 + 11.8}$

6 Which is the best estimate for 42.8×29.5?

A 40×30 B 43×27 C 43×30 D 40×26

7 Which is the best estimate for $74.81 \div 24.8$?

A $75 \div 25$ B $75 \div 20$ C $70 \div 20$ D $70 \div 25$

8 Use an estimate to show that the answers to these calculations cannot be correct.

a $64 \times 35 = 224$ b $52 \times 31 = 16\,120$

c $886 \times 610 = 54\,046$ d $4346 \div 53 = 820$

9 A bottle of spring water costs 78 p. Estimate whether £5 is enough to pay for 6 bottles.

10 A comic costs £2.95. Estimate how many you can buy for £15.

11 Robert went out for breakfast. He bought an adult breakfast for £4.99, a child's breakfast for £2.99, a carton of juice for 49 p and a black coffee for £1.79. Estimate if he got any change from £10.

12 A pack of 9 cupcakes costs £2.65 and a pack of 3 cartons of blackcurrant juice costs 87 p. Estimate if Annabelle can buy 9 cupcakes and 9 cartons of juice with £6.

Exercise 1C Using a calculator and rounding

1 Use a calculator to work out the answers to each of these calculations then round them to 1 decimal place.

a $\dfrac{648 + 324}{294 - 67}$ b $\dfrac{149 + 65}{84 \times 4}$ c $\dfrac{225 \times 43}{361 + 987}$ d $\dfrac{186 + 232}{94 + 51}$

e $\dfrac{504 + 323}{965 - 676}$ f $\dfrac{802 + 105}{65 \times 3}$ g $\dfrac{694 - 381}{657 + 101}$ h $\dfrac{64 \times 8}{512 - 128}$

2 a Estimate answers to these calculations, without using a calculator.

i $\dfrac{152 + 348}{82 - 28}$ ii $\dfrac{957 - 648}{92 - 33}$ iii $\dfrac{924 - 118}{196 \times 2}$

b Now use a calculator to work out the exact answers and round them to 1 decimal place. Were your estimates close to the answers?

3 Use a calculator to work out these calculations and round your answers to 1 decimal place.

a $72.8 \div (6.2 - 4.1)$ b $(19.3 + 5.24) \times 8.1$

c $(26.4 - 13.8) \div 4.3$ d $42.6 \times (16.8 - 9.24)$

4 Use a calculator to find answers to these calculations and round your answers to 2 decimal places.

a $756 \div 26$ b $424 \div 31$ c $841 \div 92$

d $6232 \div 17$ e $2437 \div 93$ f $2017 \div 17$

2 Number calculations

Exercise 2A Multiplying and dividing by 10, 100 and 1000

 1 Write down the answers to these calculations.

a 6×10 **b** 23×10 **c** 17×1000 **d** 4.7×100

e 8.1×10 **f** 3.4×1000 **g** $46 \div 10$ **h** $29 \div 1000$

i $65 \div 100$ **j** $7.1 \div 100$ **k** $3.8 \div 10$ **l** $5.4 \div 1000$

m 0.43×1000 **n** $7 \div 100$ **o** 0.032×100 **p** $32.8 \div 1000$

q 0.002×100 **r** $0.19 \div 100$

2 Find the missing number in each of these calculations.

a $46 \times ? = 4600$ **b** $? \div 10 = 2.3$ **c** $0.52 \times 1000 = ?$

d $8.2 \div 100 = ?$ **e** $0.04 \times ? = 40$ **f** $? \div 100 = 0.025$

g $? \div 1000 = 0.68$ **h** $0.063 \times 100 = ?$ **i** $8.65 \times ? = 86.5$

j $75 \div ? = 0.75$ **k** $? \div 100 = 9.23$ **l** $63.9 \div 10 = ?$

m $? \times 1000 = 7610$ **n** $843 \div 100 = ?$ **o** $? \times 1000 = 4.3$

p $65.3 \div ? = 0.653$ **q** $0.0813 \times 1000 = ?$ **r** $? \div 1000 = 0.902$

Exercise 2B Whole number calculations

In this exercise use a written method to calculate your answers. Show all your working.

1 Calculate.

a 23×9 **b** 74×6 **c** 56×4 **d** 9×45

e 382×5 **f** 3×115 **g** 725×11 **h** 629×8

i 6×256 **j** 386×12 **k** 8×822 **l** 12×443

2 Calculate.

a 16×52 **b** 31×45 **c** 72×28 **d** 64×32

e 81×92 **f** 59×24 **g** 218×31 **h** 453×46

i 822×51 **j** 626×62 **k** 921×54 **l** 873×46

3 Solve these division calculations.

a $148 \div 4$ **b** $966 \div 7$ **c** $318 \div 6$

d $485 \div 5$ **e** $1784 \div 8$ **f** $1848 \div 7$

4 Solve these division calculations.

Give your answers:

i with the remainder   **ii** as a decimal.

a $516 \div 8$ **b** $165 \div 6$ **c** $407 \div 5$ **d** $554 \div 4$

5 Calculate the following, writing your answer with a remainder if required.

a $871 \div 13$ **b** $1920 \div 15$ **c** $5681 \div 23$ **d** $9216 \div 18$

e $3672 \div 24$ **f** $1118 \div 18$ **g** $1300 \div 27$ **h** $1858 \div 35$

i $1497 \div 22$ **j** $2575 \div 31$

Exercise 2C Number problems

1 Find two numbers that have:

    a a sum of 10 and a product of 24   **b** a sum of 5 and a product of 6

    c a sum of 7 and a product of 12   **d** a sum of 12 and a product of 36.

2 Mo runs the 10 000 m race in the championships. One lap of the track is 400 m. How many laps did he run?

3 A group of 7 friends go out for a meal in a restaurant. The bill comes to £239. They decide that everyone will pay £35. Is this enough to pay the bill?

4 Shirley goes strawberry picking in her holidays. She picks 3760 g from one row. How many 400 g punnets does this fill? How much is left over?

5 Ian buys a new guitar costing £864. The shop allows him to pay in 12 equal monthly instalments. How much does he pay each month?

6 A single tin of beans costs 46 p. A multipack of 6 tins costs £2.25. How much do you save by buying the multipack?

7 A group of 2 adults and 3 children visit the theme park. An adult ticket costs £35 and a child's ticket costs £22. Would they save any money by buying a family ticket for £125?

8 A recipe for a batch of scones uses 400 g of flour.

    a How many batches can be made from a 6 kg bag of flour?

    b If each batch contains 12 scones, how many scones would there be in total?

> **Hint**   1000 g = 1 kg

9 The 23 pupils in register class 1G1 are taking part in the school sponsored walk. Each person raises £18. How much money does the class raise in total?

10 Ross has a collection of records which he keeps in a unit with 6 shelves. He wants to estimate the size of his collection, so he counts the records on one shelf and finds there are 86 records. If he assumes all the shelves hold the same amount, how many records does he have?

11 A seaside café sells ice cream in single cones. On one summer day the café sells 2880 ml of vanilla ice cream. A single cone contains 40 ml of ice cream. How many single cones did they sell on that day?

12 A van weighs 2.6 tonnes. To remain legal, its total weight including any load must be no more than 3.5 tonnes. Can it carry 3 crates, each weighing 305 kg? Explain your answer.

> **Hint**   1 tonne = 1000 kg

13 Three friends are going on an all-inclusive holiday to Tenerife costing £384 each.

    a How much do they pay altogether?

    b They had a budget of £1200 for their holiday. How much over or under budget were the friends?

14 A wind turbine rotates at a speed of 14 revolutions per minute. How many revolutions does it complete in 1 hour?

15 The apple trees grown by Alves Apples are planted in rows to make the apples easier to look after and to pick. There are 23 rows and each row has 18 trees. How many apple trees do they have altogether?

3 Using number facts

Exercise 3A Quick methods and estimation

1 Calculate the following.

a 4×100	**b** 4×600	**c** 4×80
d 20×300	**e** 70×40	**f** 900×30
g 120×40	**h** 80×200	**i** 700×50
j 60×3000	**k** 800×30	**l** 70×80
m 70×600	**n** 73×30	**o** 42×6000

> **Hint** To calculate 20×300, split it into $20 \times 3 \times 100$.

2 Work out the answers to these division calculations.

a $1600 \div 40$	**b** $9000 \div 30$	**c** $630 \div 90$
d $350 \div 70$	**e** $480 \div 80$	**f** $28\,000 \div 40$
g $3600 \div 200$	**h** $72\,000 \div 900$	**i** $16\,000 \div 800$
j $5600 \div 700$	**k** $7200 \div 300$	**l** $2100 \div 60$

> **Hint** To calculate $400 \div 20$, split it into $400 \div 2 \div 10$.

3 Each of these calculations has three possible answers shown. Which answer is correct?

a $60 \times 400 = ?$ 240, 2400, 24\,000   **b** $800 \times 700 = ?$ 560, 56\,000, 560\,000

c $1200 \times 30 = ?$ 3600, 36\,000, 360\,000   **d** $56\,000 \div 700 = ?$ 8, 80, 800

4 Estimate the answers to these calculations, then calculate the exact answer.

a 43×19	**b** 72×33	**c** 56×14	**d** 38×87
e $2418 \div 62$	**f** $798 \div 38$	**g** $4218 \div 57$	**h** $3630 \div 55$

Exercise 3B Using number facts

1 Given that $3 \times 6 = 18$, write down the answers to these calculations.

a 30×6	**b** 30×60	**c** 30×6000
d $18 \div 6$	**e** $180 \div 6$	**f** $1800 \div 30$

2 Given that $8 \times 7 = 56$, write down the answers to these calculations.

a 80×70	**b** $560 \div 80$	**c** 800×70
d $5600 \div 70$	**e** $5600 \div 800$	**f** 16×7

3 Given that $17 \times 8 = 136$, write down the answers to these calculations.

a 17×80	**b** $1360 \div 8$	**c** 800×170
d $1360 \div 170$	**e** 80×170	**f** 34×80

Exercise 3C Multiplying decimals

1 Use number facts to write down the answers to these calculations.

a 0.3×3 **b** 0.4×2 **c** 0.6×4 **d** 0.8×6

e 7×0.3 **f** 0.9×5 **g** 0.5×7 **h** 8×0.7

i 3×0.8 **j** 0.6×7 **k** 0.9×6 **l** 0.8×5

> **Hint** For more practice on multiplying decimals, see Chapter 8.

2 Write down the answers to these calculations.

a 0.3×0.2 **b** 0.7×0.1 **c** 0.3×0.5 **d** 0.8×0.4

e 0.6×0.7 **f** 0.9×0.9 **g** 0.6×0.9 **h** 0.4×0.8

i 0.7×0.5 **j** 0.4×0.7 **k** 0.2×0.6 **l** 0.8×0.9

3 Write down the answers to these calculations.

a 0.6×30 **b** 0.5×60 **c** 0.8×30 **d** 0.7×60

e 0.8×90 **f** 70×0.4 **g** 30×0.7 **h** 0.9×50

i 0.3×80 **j** 60×0.8 **k** 0.6×60 **l** 0.9×40

4 Write down the answers to these calculations.

a 0.5×0.03 **b** 0.07×0.6 **c** 0.9×0.05

d 0.04×0.3 **e** 0.6×0.04 **f** 0.08×0.3

5 Write down the answers to these calculations.

a 0.4×6 **b** 0.8×0.009 **c** 0.08×0.08 **d** 0.06×70

e 30×0.008 **f** 0.006×0.5 **g** 0.08×30 **h** 0.06×200

i 0.8×400 **j** 0.09×0.7 **k** 700×0.06 **l** 0.7×0.7

4 Negative numbers

Exercise 4A Comparing negative numbers

You can use the number line shown to help you with this exercise.

```
 ┬───┬───┬───┬───┬───┬───┬───┬───┬───┬───┬───┬───┬───┬───┬───┬───┬───┬───┬───┬───┬
-10  -9  -8  -7  -6  -5  -4  -3  -2  -1   0   1   2   3   4   5   6   7   8   9  10
```

1   Write down the integer(s) that are:

    a greater than −3 and less than 2   **b** less than 4 and greater than −4

    c greater than −8 and less than −3   **d** halfway between −2 and 2

    e halfway between −5 and 3   **f** halfway between −8 and −2

> **Hint**   An integer is a positive or negative whole number.

2   Which of these numbers is greater?

    a −4 or −2   **b** −3 or −5   **c** −10 or −7   **d** 0 or −2

    e −8 or 6   **f** −8 or −6   **g** 2 or −4   **h** −11 or −1

3   Write these sets of numbers in order from smallest to largest.

    a −4, 3, −1, 2, 0   **b** 6, −13, 11, −1, −8

    c −1, 10, −7, −9, 0   **d** 5, −3, 1, −5, 3

4   Copy these pairs of numbers and insert the correct sign, < or >.

    a −3 ... 1   **b** −5 ... −2   **c** 1 ... −6

    d −8 ... −11   **e** 0 ... −2   **f** −7 ... −4

    g −12 ... −10   **h** −1 ... −6

> **Hint**   < means less than, > means greater than.

Exercise 4B Adding and subtracting negative numbers

1   Work out the answers to these calculations.

    a 4 − 7   **b** 1 − 10   **c** 15 − 19   **d** 0 − 4

    e 23 − 29   **f** 14 − 24   **g** 6 − 7   **h** 8 − 20

    i 15 − 25   **j** 6 − 8   **k** 2 − 3   **l** 4 − 8

2   Calculate.

    a 3 + (−2)   **b** 7 + (−2)   **c** (−5) + (−7)

    d 12 + (−10)   **e** (−12) + (−20)   **f** 8 + (−13)

    g (−11) + (−11)   **h** (−1) + (−10)   **i** 14 + (−19)

    j 6 + (−7)   **k** 18 + (−24)   **l** (−1) + (−8)

> **Hint**   Remember: adding a negative number is the same as subtracting a positive number.

3   Calculate.

    a 2 − (−3)   **b** (−6) − (−5)   **c** (−3) − (−3)

    d (−12) − (−4)   **e** 3 − (−3)   **f** (−5) − (−6)

    g (−6) − (−2)   **h** (−17) − (−8)   **i** 5 − (−4)

    j (−11) − (−11)   **k** 1 − (−3)   **l** 6 − (−6)

> **Hint**   Remember: subtracting a negative number is the same as adding a positive number.

4 Calculate.

a 8 – 14   b (–3) – (–2)   c (–7) + (–3)   d (–1) – (–8)

e 15 – 18   f (–3) + (–2)   g 4 + (–7)   h 1 – (–3)

i 16 + (–9)   j 3 + (–4)   k (–7) – (–5)   l 2 + (–13)

m (–15) – (–15)   n (–8) + (–8)

5 Calculate.

a 2 – 6 + 4   b (–3) + 7 + (–9)   c (–12) – (–3) + 3

d 1 + (–7) – 2   e (–9) – (–12) + (–11)   f (–16) – (–20) + (–3)

g (–2) + (–2) – (–2)   h (–2) – (–2) – (–2)

Exercise 4C Negative number problems

1 Write these temperatures in order, from the coldest to the warmest.

a –5 °C, 3 °C, –11 °C, 18 °C, –3 °C   b 6 °C, –2 °C, –4 °C, –9 °C, 0 °C

c 8 °C, –3° C, 1 °C, –8 °C, –12 °C   d 1 °C, –1 °C, –7 °C, 7 °C, –4 °C

2 Write down the difference between the following pairs of temperatures.

a –3 °C, 4 °C   b 2 °C, –6 °C   c –13 °C, 5 °C   d 15 °C, –4 °C

3 The average January temperatures for five major cities are given below.

  Glasgow 1 °C   Helsinki –8 °C   Budapest –3 °C   Barcelona 4 °C   Hamburg –1 °C

a Which city has the lowest average temperature in January?

b How much warmer is Glasgow than Budapest?

c What is the difference in temperature between the coldest and warmest cities?

4 Part of a bank statement is shown below. Copy the table and complete the balance column.

Deposits (£)	Withdrawals (£)	Balance (£)
250		250
	160	
	110	
	35	
40		
20		

5   A bank statement is shown below with some of the deposits and withdrawals missing.
    Copy the table and complete the blank entries.

Deposits (£)	Withdrawals (£)	Balance (£)
300		300
		170
		−30
		25
		−80
		35

6   Katie and Matt are going out shopping. They start off with £120 in their bank account.

    They spend £75 in Parks & Sinclair then another £65 in VeryDry. Katie thinks this has
    made them overdrawn, so transfers £50 over from their savings.

    Can they then afford to spend £40 on lunch and still leave money in their account?

7   The mountain Cairn Gorm is 1245 m high and nearby Loch Ness is 230 m deep.
    What is the difference in height between the bottom of Loch Ness and the top of
    Cairn Gorm?

8   The final scores for five players in a golf tournament are shown below.

    Jon −17   Scott −13   Richie −11   David −8   Duncan −5

    a Who was the winner?

    b How many shots ahead of his nearest rival did he finish?

    c How many shots was Scott ahead of Duncan?

    Hint   In golf, the lowest score wins.

9   Lewis qualified for the Austrian Grand Prix with his fastest lap time of 1 minute
    4.424 seconds. The timings showed that Sebastian was 0.131 s faster than Lewis and
    Valtteri was 0.173 s faster than Lewis.

    a What were the qualifying times for Sebastian and Valtteri?

    b How much quicker was Valtteri than Sebastian?

5 Multiples and factors

Exercise 5A Common multiples

Example 5.1

Write down the first six multiples of 9.

9, 18, 27, 36, 45 and 54 ●————— | **Multiples** of a number appear in the times table for that number.

1. Write down the first five multiples of:

   a 2   **b** 7   **c** 6   **d** 12

2. Are these numbers multiples of 3? Explain how you know.

   a 108   **b** 316   **c** 211   **d** 510

3. Are these numbers multiples of 6? Explain how you know.

   a 102   **b** 476   **c** 624   **d** 893

Example 5.2

Find the lowest common multiple of 4 and 14.

Multiples of 4: 4, 8, 12, 16, 20, 24, (28), 32, 36 ●———— | Write out the multiples of each number.
Multiples of 14: 14, (28), 42 | The **lowest common multiple (LCM)** is the smallest number that is in both times tables.
LCM of 4 and 14 is 28.

4. Find the lowest common multiple of the following pairs of numbers.

   a 3 and 5   **b** 6 and 15   **c** 9 and 12   **d** 8 and 18

   e 7 and 12   **f** 4 and 18   **g** 6 and 9   **h** 6 and 16

5. Find the lowest common multiple of the following sets of numbers.

   a 2, 5 and 6   **b** 4, 6 and 15   **c** 5, 9 and 12   **d** 4, 6 and 9

   e 8, 9 and 12   **f** 2, 5 and 7   **g** 6, 8 and 15   **h** 3, 4 and 13

6. Recycling bins are collected on a rolling schedule, with the bin for paper being collected every 2 weeks and the bin for plastics collected every 3 weeks. If they were both collected this week, how long will it be until they are next collected in the same week?

7. Alex completes a lap of a cross-country running track in 6 minutes and Francis completes it in 8 minutes. If they both start together, how long will it be until they cross the line at the same time?

8. Joe visits the gym every 4 days, goes to the cinema once a week and walks to work every second day. If he did all three things today, how many days will it be until he does them all on the same day again?

9. The number 11 bus runs every 30 minutes during the day, the number 33C runs every 18 minutes and the number 32 runs every 10 minutes. They are all at the bus station at 4:00 pm. What is the next time they will be at the bus station together?

Exercise 5B Common factors

Example 5.3

Find all the factors of 30.

1, 2, 3, 5, 6, 10, 15 and 30 •———— The **factors** of a number divide into it exactly. They appear in **factor pairs**. For example, 5 × 6 = 30 so 5 and 6 are both factors of 30.

 1 Find all the factors of the following numbers.

a 24   b 28   c 45   d 56

2 One factor of each of the following numbers is given. Find its partner in its factor pair.

a One factor of 72 is 9.   b One factor of 108 is 4.

c One factor of 437 is 19.   d One factor of 196 is 14.

Example 5.4

Find the highest common factor of 12 and 32.

The factors of 12 are: 1, 2, 3, ④, 6, 12
The factors of 32 are: 1, 2, ④, 8, 16, 32
The highest common factor is 4.

•———— Write out the factors of 12 and 32. The **highest common factor (HCF)** is the largest number that is a factor of both numbers, that is, it appears in both lists of factors.

3 Use your answers from Question 1 to find the highest common factor of:

a 24 and 28   b 24 and 56   c 24 and 45   d 28 and 56

4 Find the highest common factor of these pairs of numbers.

a 27 and 36   b 40 and 72   c 36 and 84   d 64 and 96

e 35 and 91   f 26 and 39   g 24 and 96   h 20 and 39

 5 Mr MacLeod has 36 square concrete slabs he wants to use to make a rectangular patio in his garden. One way he could arrange them is to make a rectangle with length of 9 slabs and breadth of 4 slabs, as shown.

In how many different ways can he arrange the 36 slabs to make a rectangular patio?

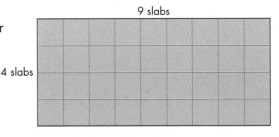

9 slabs

4 slabs

 6 A warehouse has a security keypad that will open the door if you type in the correct 4-digit code. Some clues to remember the code are given below.

- The first two digits are the highest common factor of 32 and 80.

- The third and fourth digits are the highest common factor of 28 and 98.

What is the code to open the door?

6 Primes and prime factors

Exercise 6A Prime numbers and prime factors

Example 6.1

Which of these numbers is prime?

a 39   **b** 23

> **Hint** A prime number is a number that has exactly two factors, itself and 1.

a $1 \times 39 = 39$ ──── List all the factor pairs to make 39.

    $3 \times 13 = 39$

  39 has more than two factors so it is not prime.

b $1 \times 23 = 23$

  23 is prime because it has exactly two factors.

 1 Write down all the factor pairs of the following numbers. State whether each number is 'prime' or 'not prime'.

    a 21   **b** 31   **c** 41   **d** 51

Example 6.2

Write 24 as a product of prime factors using:

a a prime factor tree   **b** the division method.

a
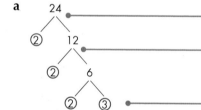

Split 24 into 2×12. 2 is a prime number so circle it.

Split 12 into 2×6 and then split 6 into 2×3.

Stop here because 2 and 3 are prime numbers. You can start with any factor pairs, but must end up with prime numbers at the end of each branch.

So, $24 = 2 \times 2 \times 2 \times 3$ ──── Write 24 as a product of its prime factors.

b
```
2 | 24
2 | 12
2 | 6
3 | 3
    1
```

Repeatedly divide by a prime factor (here 2, and then 3). Stop when you reach 1.

So, $24 = 2 \times 2 \times 2 \times 3$

 2 Use a prime factor tree to find the prime factors of:

    a 26   **b** 18   **c** 36   **d** 48   **e** 30

    f 50   **g** 84   **h** 360   **i** 78   **j** 63

 3 Use the division method to find the prime factors of:

    a 14   **b** 56   **c** 66   **d** 150   **e** 210

4 Use your preferred method to write the following numbers as a product of prime factors.

a 68	**b** 294	**c** 280	**d** 525	**e** 98
f 132	**g** 234	**h** 364	**i** 660	**j** 156

Exercise 6B Using prime factors

Example 6.3

Use prime factors to find the highest common factor and lowest common multiple of 60 and 90.

Using prime factors, 60 = 2 × ⟨2 × 3 × 5⟩ and 90 = ⟨2 × 3 × 5⟩ × 3

> You can see that 2 × 3 × 5 is common to both lists of prime factors, so write 2, 3 and 5 in the intersection (overlap).

60   90
2   2   3
     3
     5

> Write the remaining prime factors of 60 in the left outside part and the remaining prime factors of 90 in the right outside part.

2 × 3 × 5 = 30, so 30 is the highest common factor

> The product of the numbers in the intersection is the highest common factor.

2 × 2 × 3 × 5 × 3 = 180, so 180 is the lowest common multiple

> The product of all the numbers inside both rings (including the intersection) is the lowest common multiple.

1 Using the diagrams below, work out the highest common factor and lowest common multiple of each pair of numbers.

a 16   18
2   2   3
2   3
2

b 18   24
3   2   2
     3   2

c 45   60
3   3   2
     5   2

2 The prime factors of a pair of numbers are given below. Put these into a diagram like those in Question 1 and use the diagram to find the highest common factor and lowest common multiple of each pair.

a 18 = 2 × 3 × 3
   30 = 2 × 3 × 5

b 18 = 2 × 3 × 3
   48 = 2 × 2 × 2 × 2 × 3

c 18 = 2 × 3 × 3
   45 = 3 × 3 × 5

3 Find the highest common factor and lowest common multiple of these pairs of numbers.

a 30 and 48	**b** 24 and 60	**c** 63 and 84
d 40 and 84	**e** 63 and 210	**f** 132 and 234
g 50 and 525	**h** 98 and 539	**i** 294 and 364

7 Powers and index form

Exercise 7A Index form

Example 7.1

a Write $5 \times 5 \times 5 \times 5$ in index form.   **b** Write 8^3 in expanded form and evaluate it.

a $5 \times 5 \times 5 \times 5 = 5^4$ •——————

> There are four 5s being multiplied together, so 5 is the base number and 4 is the power.

b $8^3 = 8 \times 8 \times 8$ •————

    $= 512$

> The base number is 8 and the power is 3, so write it as three 8s multiplied together. **Evaluate** means work out the answer.

1   Write these expressions in index form.

    a $2 \times 2 \times 2$ **b** $4 \times 4 \times 4 \times 4 \times 4$

    c 7×7 **d** $5 \times 5 \times 5 \times 5$

    e $3 \times 3 \times 3 \times 3 \times 3$ **f** $2 \times 2 \times 2 \times 2 \times 2 \times 2$

    g $9 \times 9 \times 9 \times 9$ **h** $1 \times 1 \times 1 \times 1 \times 1 \times 1 \times 1$

    i $11 \times 11 \times 11$ **j** $8 \times 8 \times 8 \times 8 \times 8 \times 8$

    k 3 **l** $k \times k \times k \times k$

    m $a \times a \times a$ **n** $n \times n \times n \times n \times n \times n \times n \times n$

2   Calculate the following, showing the necessary working.

    a 6^2 **b** 4^3 **c** 2^6 **d** 3^4 **e** 5^4

    f 2^8 **g** 7^3 **h** 1^7 **i** 4^1 **j** 0^3

    k 4^4 **l** 10^3 **m** 8^3 **n** 1^{10} **o** 2^{10}

3   Write the following expressions in index form.

    a $2 \times 2 \times 2 \times 5$ **b** $3 \times 3 \times 7 \times 7$

    c $2 \times 2 \times 3 \times 5 \times 2$ **d** $3 \times 3 \times 5 \times 3 \times 5 \times 3$

    e $2 \times 3 \times 3 \times 3 \times 5 \times 2 \times 5 \times 5 \times 5 \times 3$ **f** $5 \times 3 \times 2 \times 6 \times 6 \times 6 \times 2 \times 6 \times 6$

    g $5 \times 7 \times 10 \times 10 \times 7 \times 5 \times 10 \times 10 \times 5 \times 10$ **h** $a \times b \times a \times b$

    i $y \times z \times z \times z \times y \times y \times z$ **j** $j \times k \times j \times k \times l \times k \times l$

4   Calculate the following.

    a $4^3 + 3^2$ **b** $2^4 + 4^2$ **c** $3^3 - 2^2$ **d** $5^3 - 3^3$

    e $2^3 + 3^2 + 4^2$ **f** $2^3 + 3^3 - 4^2$ **g** $10^3 - 3^3 - 5^2$ **h** $4^3 + 2^3 - 6^2$

    i $10^2 - 9^2 - 4^2$ **j** $3^3 + 7^2 - 2^6$

5   The area A of a square is given by the formula $A = l^2$, where l is the length of the sides. Calculate the area, in cm², of squares with these side lengths.

    a 3 cm   **b** 6 cm   **c** 10 cm   **d** 7 cm   **e** 15 cm

6   The volume V of a cube is given by the formula $V = l^3$, where l is the length of the sides. Calculate the volume, in cm³, of cubes with these side lengths.

    a 5 cm   **b** 7 cm   **c** 8 cm   **d** 9 cm   **e** 11 cm

Exercise 7B Using a calculator 🖩

Use a calculator for these questions.

1 Calculate.

    a 4^5 **b** 3^6 **c** 5^4 **d** 7^7 **e** 9^4

    f 3^9 **g** 10^6 **h** 5^7 **i** 4^9 **j** 2^{20}

2 Calculate the following.

    a $2^6 \times 5^5$ **b** $3^4 \times 7^3$ **c** $5^7 - 7^5$ **d** $2^8 + 3^5$

    e $5^6 - 6^5$ **f** $3^3 + 5^5 + 7^7$ **g** $10^4 - 3^7 + 6^6$ **h** $2^8 - 3^8 + 5^8$

    i $10^5 - 2^{10} - 3^{10}$ **j** $7^6 - 5^6 - 10^5$

3 Calculate the following, rounding your answers to 2 decimal places when required.

    a $\dfrac{2^5 + 4^4}{2^6}$ **b** $\dfrac{4^6 - 3^5}{5^2}$ **c** $\dfrac{7^5 - 10^4}{3^6}$ **d** $\dfrac{8^4 + 6^5}{11^3}$

    e $\dfrac{6^4 + 4^3}{5^3 + 7^3}$ **f** $\dfrac{7^6 + 8^4}{5^6 - 4^4}$ **g** $\dfrac{8^6 - 5^7}{6^4 + 3^6}$ **h** $\dfrac{9^5 - 6^4}{10^5 - 8^3}$

> **Hint**   If your calculator doesn't have a fractions button, then put brackets around the numerator and around the denominator when you enter these calculations to ensure they are worked out correctly.

8 Calculating with fractions, decimals and percentages

Exercise 8A Converting between fractions, decimal fractions and percentages

1 Write each of the following fractions as:

i a decimal   **ii** a percentage.

a $\frac{1}{2}$ **b** $\frac{1}{10}$ **c** $\frac{1}{4}$ **d** $\frac{1}{3}$

e $\frac{7}{10}$ **f** $\frac{3}{5}$ **g** $\frac{23}{100}$ **h** $\frac{5}{8}$

> **Hint** To convert a fraction to a decimal, write it as an equivalent fraction with a denominator of 100 then divide the numerator by 100.
> The numerator of the fraction gives the percentage.

2 Write each of these decimals as:

i a fraction   **ii** a percentage.

Write your fractions in their simplest form.

a 0.75   **b** 0.23   **c** 0.85   **d** 0.03

e 0.62   **f** 0.9   **g** 0.36   **h** 0.175

> **Hint** To convert a decimal to a fraction, write it as an equivalent fraction with a denominator of 100 then simplify.
> Multiply the decimal by 100 to write it as a percentage.

3 Write each of these percentages as:

i a decimal   **ii** a fraction.

Write your fractions in their simplest form.

a 40%   **b** 72%   **c** 16%   **d** 7%

e 44%   **f** 83%   **g** 96%   **h** $66\frac{2}{3}\%$

> **Hint** To convert a percentage to a decimal, divide it by 100. Write it as an equivalent fraction with a denominator of 100 then simplify to find the fraction.

4 Which of these numbers is the largest: 0.38, $\frac{3}{8}$ or 35%?

> **Hint** Write them all in the same form so you can compare them.

Exercise 8B Adding and subtracting decimals

1. Calculate the following, showing your working as appropriate.

   a 4.2 + 6.5   **b** 12.8 − 4.7   **c** 6.4 + 2.9

   d 16.4 − 8.6   **e** 3.3 + 5.7 + 6.9   **f** 21.5 + 2.8 − 18.2

   g 15.4 − 8.1 + 3.8   **h** 32.4 − 24.7 − 6.6   **i** 19.3 cm + 1.1 cm − 8.5 cm

   j 4.9 kg + 8.6 kg + 6.4 kg   **k** 11.7 m − 6.5 m + 1.4 m   **l** 16.3 cm − 9.1 cm − 2.7 cm

2. Work out the following.

   a 6.248 + 5.135   **b** 19.549 − 6.124   **c** 4.35 + 8.12 + 3.56

   d 21.9 + 8.32 − 6.47   **e** 15.54 − 6.82 − 8.43   **f** 21.92 + 8.4 − 16.88

   g 41.95 − 23.06 − 6.7   **h** 66.5 − 37.88 − 19.06   **i** 94.85 − 75.938 − 18.6

   j 45.045 + 26 − 31.7   **k** 24.764 + 32.912 − 7.8 − 18.48   **l** 6.125 − 4.3 + 3.1415 − 0.04 + 8.1

3. A small lorry is legally allowed to have a total weight of 7.5 tonnes, including its load. The weight of the lorry alone is 3200 kg. What is the maximum weight of cargo, in tonnes, it can legally carry?

   > **Hint**   1 tonne = 1000 kg

4. A car's fuel tank holds 55.2 litres. On a journey from Forres to Aberdeen, 13.84 litres of fuel were used. If the tank was full at the start of the journey, how much fuel was left?

5. In a coffee shop, a medium Americano costs £2.45, a pot of tea costs £2.35 and a cola costs £2.75. What is the total cost of these three drinks?

6. Ali ordered a batch of 750 kg of concrete to make a base for a new shed.

   a He used 712.64 kg to make the base. How much concrete was left over?

   b He wants to use the left-over concrete to put up 4 fence posts. Each post needs 10 kg of concrete. Does he have enough left for all 4 posts?

7. A magazine costs £4.95, a packet of sweets is 79 p, a sandwich is £1.75 and a bottle of water costs 85 p. What is the total cost of all four items?

8. A recipe for a Thai curry includes 0.8 kg of pork, 225 g of shallots, 0.025 kg of fresh ginger, 50 g of peanuts and 0.055 kg of sugar. What is the total weight of these ingredients, in kilograms?

Exercise 8C Multiplying decimals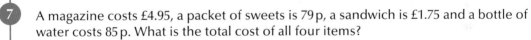

1. Use the fact that 23 × 68 = 1564 to write down the answers to these calculations.

   a 2.3 × 68   **b** 23 × 6.8   **c** 2.3 × 6.8   **d** 0.23 × 0.68

2. Use the fact that 78 × 55 = 4290 to write down the answers to these calculations.

   a 7.8 × 55   **b** 7.8 × 5.5   **c** 5.5 × 0.78   **d** 0.78 × 55

3. Write down the answers to the following calculations.

   a 0.6 × 6   **b** 0.4 × 9   **c** 2 × 0.8   **d** 0.9 × 9

   e 0.6 × 0.3   **f** 0.7 × 0.4   **g** 0.5 × 0.8   **h** 0.4 × 0.9

   i 0.4 × 0.07   **j** 0.09 × 0.2   **k** 0.6 × 0.05   **l** 0.07 × 0.003

4 Write down the answers to these calculations.

   a 0.6×10 **b** 0.2×100 **c** 10×0.9 **d** 0.08×100

   e 0.4×30 **f** 0.9×20 **g** 0.08×20 **h** 50×0.03

   i 0.02×50 **j** 0.03×60 **k** 500×0.007 **l** 0.003×60

5 Calculate the following.

   a 5.3×6 **b** 7.1×8 **c** 4.62×6 **d** 3.14×9

   e 23.7×5 **f** 66.2×8 **g** 84.2×6 **h** 57.3×3

   i 4.2×3.4 **j** 8.1×4.6 **k** 5.3×4.7 **l** 12.6×7.4

6 One grain of rice weighs approximately 0.016 grams. How much would 5000 grains weigh?

Exercise 8D Dividing decimals

1 State the answers to the following calculations.

   a $0.8 \div 4$ **b** $0.6 \div 2$ **c** $2.4 \div 6$ **d** $7.2 \div 9$

   e $3.2 \div 8$ **f** $8.1 \div 9$ **g** $4.8 \div 8$ **h** $4.9 \div 7$

2 Write down the answers to these calculations.

   a $0.32 \div 4$ **b** $0.88 \div 8$ **c** $0.72 \div 9$ **d** $0.42 \div 6$

   e $0.49 \div 7$ **f** $0.18 \div 3$ **g** $0.28 \div 7$ **h** $0.65 \div 5$

3 Calculate each of the following.

   a $6.84 \div 2$ **b** $8.28 \div 4$ **c** $11.15 \div 5$ **d** $1.62 \div 6$

   e $11.97 \div 9$ **f** $16.86 \div 3$ **g** $21.98 \div 7$ **h** $54.56 \div 8$

4 Calculate each of the following.

   a $16.28 \div 2$ **b** $27.66 \div 3$ **c** $28.32 \div 8$ **d** $24.06 \div 3$

   e $20.16 \div 6$ **f** $52.57 \div 7$ **g** $47.88 \div 9$ **h** $36.2 \div 5$

   i $34.65 \div 7$ **j** $14.3 \div 5$ **k** $77.44 \div 8$ **l** $27.4 \div 4$

5 A medium pepperoni pizza contains 62.4 grams of protein. If it is cut into 8 equal slices, how many grams of protein are in each slice?

6 The perimeter of a regular hexagon is 26.1 cm. What is the length of each side?

> **Hint**   A regular hexagon has all sides the same length.

Exercise 8E Fractions of quantities

 1 Find each of these.

a $\frac{3}{4}$ of £28

b $\frac{2}{3}$ of 36 km

c $\frac{3}{7}$ of 42 minutes

d $\frac{2}{5}$ of £65

e $\frac{5}{9}$ of 540 g

f $\frac{5}{8}$ of 56 people

g $\frac{5}{6}$ of 42 litres

h $\frac{3}{10}$ of 1500 m

i $\frac{5}{12}$ of 84 miles

j $\frac{4}{5}$ of 95 cars

k $\frac{7}{8}$ of £36

l $\frac{5}{11}$ of 132 kg

m $\frac{5}{12}$ of 720°

n $\frac{4}{9}$ of 108 seconds

o $\frac{11}{15}$ of 450 ml

> **Hint** To find a fraction of an amount, multiply the amount by the fraction.

 2 A pair of trousers costing £56 were on sale for $\frac{3}{4}$ of their original price.

How much did they cost in the sale?

3 A promotional box of chocolates had an extra $\frac{2}{3}$ free. The original box contained 240 g of chocolates. How much extra was in the promotional box?

4 Jack has been training for the 200 m sprint. Before training, he completed the 200 m in 45 s. After training he reduced his time by $\frac{3}{10}$.

By how many seconds has he reduced his time?

5 A full can of fizzy juice contains 330 ml. Jenny has drunk $\frac{3}{5}$ of her can.

How many millilitres of juice does she have left?

6 In a survey, $\frac{5}{8}$ of the 520 people asked said they preferred 'BrytSudz' washing powder.

How many people preferred the 'BrytSudz' brand?

Exercise 8F Multiplying fractions

Example 8.1

Calculate $\frac{1}{2} \times \frac{3}{8}$

$\frac{1}{2} \times \frac{3}{8} = \frac{1 \times 3}{2 \times 8}$ — Multiply the numerators together, then multiply the denominators together.

$= \frac{3}{16}$ — Write as a fraction. Simplify your answer if possible.

1 Calculate the following, simplifying your answers where possible.

a $\frac{3}{4} \times \frac{4}{5}$ b $\frac{2}{5} \times \frac{2}{7}$ c $\frac{2}{3} \times \frac{3}{8}$ d $\frac{9}{10} \times \frac{5}{6}$ e $\frac{2}{3} \times \frac{7}{8}$

f $\frac{4}{9} \times \frac{9}{10}$ g $\frac{5}{9} \times \frac{7}{8}$ h $\frac{1}{2}$ of $\frac{3}{4}$ i $\frac{1}{8}$ of $\frac{4}{5}$ j $\frac{2}{5}$ of $\frac{5}{8}$

2 Calculate the following, simplifying your answers where possible.

a $2 \times \frac{2}{5}$ b $3 \times \frac{2}{9}$ c $6 \times \frac{1}{9}$ d $\frac{3}{8} \times 6$ e $\frac{9}{14} \times 7$

f $\frac{7}{8} \times 16$ g $\frac{3}{10} \times 15$ h $\frac{3}{10}$ of 25 i $\frac{5}{8}$ of 32 j $\frac{3}{7}$ of 12

3 Calculate the following, giving your answers in simplest form where possible.

a $\frac{1}{2} \times \frac{3}{4} \times \frac{1}{3}$ b $\frac{3}{8} \times \frac{2}{5} \times \frac{2}{3}$ c $\frac{5}{6} \times \frac{1}{4} \times \frac{2}{9}$ d $\frac{6}{7} \times \frac{1}{8} \times \frac{2}{5}$

e $\frac{1}{4} \times \frac{1}{4} \times \frac{1}{4}$ f $\frac{3}{4} \times \frac{5}{8} \times 32$ g $\frac{1}{2}$ of $\frac{1}{2}$ of $\frac{1}{2}$ h $\frac{2}{5}$ of $\frac{1}{8}$ of 15

4 Andrew spends $\frac{1}{6}$ of his weekly wage on food and $\frac{3}{5}$ of this is on fresh fruit and vegetables. How much of his total weekly wage is spent on fruit and vegetables?

5 A trip to Inverness used $\frac{3}{10}$ of a tank of fuel. If the tank holds 65 litres, how much fuel was used?

6 A child's ticket to the theatre costs $\frac{5}{8}$ of the full adult price of £30. Calculate the price of a child's ticket.

7 In the wildlife park, $\frac{1}{4}$ of the animals are birds and $\frac{5}{6}$ of these birds are endangered in the wild. What fraction of all the animals are endangered birds?

Exercise 8G Writing one quantity as a percentage of another

Example 8.2

Without using a calculator, write 16 out of 20 as a percentage.

16 out of 20 = $\frac{16}{20}$ (Write the first number as a fraction of the second.)

= $\frac{80}{100}$ (Change it to the equivalent fraction with 100 as the denominator by multiplying both numerator and denominator by 5.)

= 80% (The value of the numerator gives the percentage.)

 1 Without using a calculator, express the first quantity as a percentage of the second.

a 35 out of 50 b 6 out of 10 c 24 out of 25 d 65 out of 100

e 11 out of 20 f 39 out of 50 g 4 out of 10 h 42 out of 100

i 19 out of 25 j 13 out of 20

2 In a survey, 25 cat owners were asked which type of cat food their cats preferred. 14 owners said that their cats preferred Brand A cat food, 9 said their cats preferred Brand B and the rest expressed no preference. Write down the percentage of people who said:

   i Brand A   **ii** Brand B   **iii** no preference.

3 Mark scored 23 out of 25 for his chemistry test, 42 out of 50 for history and 18 out of 20 for maths.

   a Write each of his scores as a percentage.

   b In which subject did he get his best result?

4 Use a calculator to express the first quantity as a percentage of the second. Round your answers to 1 decimal place if necessary.

   a 24 out of 40   **b** 52 out of 60   **c** 62 out of 85   **d** 28 out of 35

   e 13 out of 45   **f** 75 out of 120   **g** 108 out of 140   **h** 200 out of 320

   i 34 out of 165   **j** 3 out of 285

5 A nursery group held a raffle to raise funds for new equipment and sold a total of 220 tickets. Of these, 95 were blue tickets, 72 were green and 53 were pink. Write each colour as a percentage of the tickets sold.

6 A group of 2000 motorists were asked to complete an online survey to determine which feature they found most important when picking a new car. 624 chose safety, 412 chose comfort, 752 chose fuel economy and 212 chose brand reputation. Write each of these choices as a percentage of the motorists surveyed.

Exercise 8H Percentages of quantities

1 Calculate.

   a 10% of 150   **b** 50% of 140   **c** 1% of 650   **d** 20% of 65

   e 5% of 240   **f** 25% of 160   **g** 60% of 120   **h** 40% of 40

   i 75% of 320   **j** 20% of 80   **k** 2% of 650

   l 30% of 150   **m** 25% of 250   **n** 90% of 60

   > **Hint**   Work out 10% and use multiples or fractions of 10%.

2 Work out each of the following.

   a 35% of 440   **b** 6% of 180   **c** 15% of 64   **d** 42% of 290

   e 19% of 480   **f** 4% of 60   **g** 24% of 90   **h** 52% of 920

   i 81% of 124   **j** 8% of 144

3 A visit to the cinema lasted for 2 hours. 15% of this time was spent watching the adverts before the film started. How long, in minutes, did the adverts last?

4 Calculate the following, rounding your answers where necessary.

   a 27% of 60 g   **b** 63% of £190   **c** 74% of 150 seconds

   d 33% of 360°   **e** 62% of 420 mm   **f** 47% of 95 minutes

   g 18% of £359   **h** 43% of 628 pupils   **i** 92% of 1320 kg

   j 57% of 814 trees   **k** 6% of 1359 visitors   **l** 36% of 1609 m

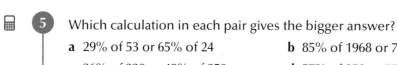

5 Which calculation in each pair gives the bigger answer?

   a 29% of 53 or 65% of 24   **b** 85% of 1968 or 75% of 2230

   c 36% of 330 or 48% of 250   **d** 57% of 950 or 75% of 720

6 38% of the 524 cars that passed the front of Simon's house in 1 hour were white. How many cars were white?

7 A tube of chocolate sweets provides 28% of the recommended daily allowance of 90 grams of sugars. How many grams of sugar does the tube contain?

Exercise 8I Percentage increase and decrease

Example 8.3

A jacket costing £64 is increased in price by 25%. Calculate its new price.

25% of 64 = 64 ÷ 4 = 16   First calculate 25% of 64. 25% is the same as $\frac{1}{4}$

64 + 16 = £80   The price has **increased**, so **add** this amount to the original price.

1 A suit costing £120 is reduced by 20% in a sale.

   a By how much has the suit been reduced?

   b What is the sale price of the suit?

2 The value of a painting bought for £540 has increased by 25% over the last year.

   a By how much did its value increase?

   b What is the painting worth now?

3 Work out the final amount when:

   a £140 is increased by 10%   **b** £350 is decreased by 20%

   c £500 is increased by 40%   **d** £240 is decreased by 25%

   e £750 is decreased by 50%   **f** £48.50 is decreased by 10%

   g £13.20 is increased by 5%   **h** £12.90 is decreased by 20%.

4 A new type of fuel claims to increase the efficiency of a car engine by 15%. If the car currently does 48 miles per gallon, what will its performance be using the new fuel?

5 The rainfall in Elgin was 60 mm in March and it increased by 34% in April.

   a By how much did the rainfall increase?

   b What was the rainfall in April?

6 Mac bought a new car for £25 000. A year later it had lost 23% of its value.

   a By how much has its value decreased?

   b What is his car now worth?

7 Work out the final amount when:

a £150 is increased by 12%   b £4520 is decreased by 28%

c £460 is increased by 36%   d £1950 is increased by 83%

e £499 is decreased by 16%   f £773 is increased by 7%

g £198 is decreased by 19%   h £545 is decreased by 42%.

 8 The number of people walking to school each day has increased by 8% over the past year. Last year, 482 people walked to school. How many walked to school this year? Round your answer appropriately.

Exercise 8J Real-life problems

1 A pair of jeans is being sold in TopWear for £90 with 30% off. The same pair of jeans is on offer in Fisco's for $\frac{1}{3}$ off the ticket price of £87.

a Which shop is offering the better deal?

b How much cheaper are the jeans in the shop offering the better deal?

2 The number of pupils in the High School has increased by $\frac{1}{10}$ from 920.

In the same town, the number of pupils in the Academy increased by 4% from 975. Which school had the bigger increase in numbers?

3 In 2015, the total amount of electricity used in Scotland was 37259 GWh. The amount generated by renewable sources was 21983 GWh. What percentage of electricity was generated by renewable sources in 2015? Round your answer appropriately.

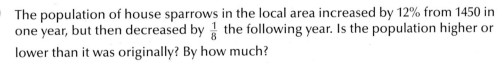

> Hint GWh is the abbreviation for Gigawatt hours, a unit used to measure energy.

4 Which would you prefer to have: 28% of £82 or $\frac{7}{9}$ of £28?

5 This season, United won 15 out of the 36 matches they played and Saints won 17 of their 38 matches. Which team had the higher winning percentage?

6 Two shops are offering a deal on a pair of shoes costing £68. ShoeWorld is offering a reduction of 36% and FootPad has $\frac{3}{8}$ off all their prices.

a Which shop has the lower selling price?

b What is the difference in their sale prices?

7 The population of house sparrows in the local area increased by 12% from 1450 in one year, but then decreased by $\frac{1}{8}$ the following year. Is the population higher or lower than it was originally? By how much?

8 The value of a painting increased by $\frac{2}{5}$ in the last year from £875. An abstract sculpture increased in value by 18% from £1250.

a Which piece of art increased more in value?

b What are the current values of these objects?

c If these increases continued at the same rates, what would their values be in another year?

9 Adding and subtracting fractions

Exercise 9A Adding and subtracting fractions with a common denominator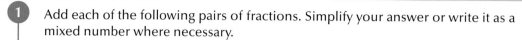

1 Add each of the following pairs of fractions. Simplify your answer or write it as a mixed number where necessary.

   a $\frac{1}{5}+\frac{2}{5}$ **b** $\frac{1}{6}+\frac{1}{6}$ **c** $\frac{2}{7}+\frac{2}{7}$ **d** $\frac{1}{9}+\frac{2}{9}$ **e** $\frac{1}{8}+\frac{3}{8}$

   f $\frac{3}{10}+\frac{3}{10}$ **g** $\frac{5}{8}+\frac{1}{8}$ **h** $\frac{7}{12}+\frac{1}{12}$ **i** $\frac{3}{5}+\frac{3}{5}$ **j** $\frac{5}{8}+\frac{7}{8}$

2 Subtract each of the following pairs of fractions. Simplify your answer or write it as a mixed number where necessary.

   a $\frac{3}{5}-\frac{2}{5}$ **b** $\frac{5}{8}-\frac{3}{8}$ **c** $\frac{4}{7}-\frac{2}{7}$ **d** $\frac{7}{9}-\frac{4}{9}$ **e** $\frac{7}{10}-\frac{3}{10}$

   f $\frac{11}{12}-\frac{5}{12}$ **g** $\frac{6}{7}-\frac{2}{7}$ **h** $\frac{8}{9}-\frac{7}{9}$ **i** $\frac{7}{20}-\frac{5}{20}$ **j** $\frac{4}{15}-\frac{1}{15}$

3 Calculate the following, simplifying your answer or writing as a mixed number where necessary.

   a $\frac{2}{9}+\frac{4}{9}$ **b** $\frac{11}{12}-\frac{7}{12}$ **c** $\frac{13}{15}-\frac{7}{15}$ **d** $\frac{7}{10}+\frac{1}{10}$

   e $\frac{6}{11}+\frac{7}{11}$ **f** $\frac{11}{12}-\frac{1}{12}$ **g** $\frac{7}{8}+\frac{5}{8}$ **h** $\frac{8}{9}-\frac{5}{9}$

   i $\frac{14}{15}-\frac{11}{15}$ **j** $\frac{9}{10}+\frac{7}{10}$ **k** $\frac{4}{5}+\frac{4}{5}$ **l** $\frac{13}{18}-\frac{7}{18}$

   m $\frac{1}{2}+\frac{1}{2}+\frac{1}{2}$ **n** $\frac{5}{8}+\frac{3}{8}+\frac{7}{8}$ **o** $\frac{7}{9}+\frac{5}{9}+\frac{7}{9}$

4 Calculate the following, simplifying your answer or writing as a mixed number where necessary.

   a $3-\frac{3}{4}$ **b** $2-\frac{5}{8}$ **c** $5-\frac{5}{9}$ **d** $4-\frac{3}{8}$ **e** $1-\frac{5}{9}$

5 Max and Robert were painting their room. When they were finished, they each had $\frac{2}{7}$ of a tin of paint left over. If they mixed their tins together, what fraction of a tin would they have left?

6 In a relay race, Ben ran $\frac{5}{7}$ of a kilometre, Sarah ran $\frac{6}{7}$ km and Scott ran $\frac{3}{7}$ km. How far was the race?

7 Erinn got a box containing 20 chocolates for her birthday. She ate 6 and gave 3 each to Peter and Ailsa. What fraction of the box was left? Simplify your answer.

Exercise 9B Adding and subtracting fractions with different denominators

Example 9.1

Calculate $\frac{1}{2} + \frac{2}{5}$

LCM of 2 and 5 is 10 •———[First find the LCM of the denominators, 2 and 5.]

$\frac{1}{2} = \frac{5}{10}$ and $\frac{2}{5} = \frac{4}{10}$ •———[Change each fraction to the equivalent fraction with the LCM as its denominator.]

$\frac{1}{2} + \frac{2}{5} = \frac{5}{10} + \frac{4}{10}$ •———[Complete the calculation using the equivalent fractions. Simplify if possible.]

$= \frac{9}{10}$

Hint Look back at Chapter 6 for more information about finding the LCM of two numbers.

1 Find the lowest common multiple of the following pairs of numbers.

    a 4, 8   **b** 6, 12   **c** 3, 6   **d** 3, 9   **e** 5, 10

    f 3, 15   **g** 2, 8   **h** 2, 4   **i** 4, 12   **j** 2, 6

2 Add these fractions. You may find your answers to Question 1 help.

    a $\frac{1}{4} + \frac{3}{8}$ **b** $\frac{5}{12} + \frac{1}{6}$ **c** $\frac{1}{6} + \frac{2}{3}$ **d** $\frac{4}{9} + \frac{1}{3}$ **e** $\frac{2}{5} + \frac{3}{10}$

    f $\frac{4}{15} + \frac{2}{3}$ **g** $\frac{3}{8} + \frac{1}{2}$ **h** $\frac{1}{2} + \frac{3}{4}$ **i** $\frac{5}{12} + \frac{1}{4}$ **j** $\frac{1}{2} + \frac{5}{6}$

3 Subtract these fractions. You may find your answers to Question 1 help.

    a $\frac{3}{8} - \frac{1}{4}$ **b** $\frac{5}{12} - \frac{1}{6}$ **c** $\frac{2}{3} - \frac{1}{6}$ **d** $\frac{4}{9} - \frac{1}{3}$ **e** $\frac{2}{5} - \frac{3}{10}$

    f $\frac{2}{3} - \frac{4}{15}$ **g** $\frac{1}{2} - \frac{3}{8}$ **h** $\frac{3}{4} - \frac{1}{2}$ **i** $\frac{5}{12} - \frac{1}{4}$ **j** $\frac{5}{6} - \frac{1}{2}$

4 Find the solutions to the following calculations.

    a $\frac{7}{12} + \frac{1}{5}$ **b** $\frac{3}{8} - \frac{1}{6}$ **c** $\frac{4}{9} + \frac{1}{2}$ **d** $\frac{1}{2} + \frac{4}{5}$

    e $\frac{2}{3} - \frac{1}{5}$ **f** $\frac{3}{5} + \frac{3}{4}$ **g** $\frac{6}{7} - \frac{1}{4}$ **h** $\frac{5}{9} + \frac{2}{3}$

    i $\frac{5}{8} + \frac{4}{7}$ **j** $\frac{7}{10} - \frac{2}{3}$ **k** $\frac{7}{5} - \frac{1}{4}$ **l** $\frac{1}{2} + \frac{1}{3} + \frac{1}{4}$

    m $\frac{5}{8} + \frac{1}{6} - \frac{1}{2}$ **n** $\frac{9}{10} - \frac{1}{4} + \frac{1}{3}$ **o** $\frac{1}{2} - \frac{1}{9} - \frac{1}{3}$ **p** $\frac{3}{5} + \frac{2}{3} - \frac{1}{4}$

5 During the weekend, Daniel played football for $\frac{1}{8}$ of his time on Saturday and $\frac{3}{16}$ of his time on Sunday. What fraction of his weekend did he spend playing football?

6 The ice cream shop makes different flavours of ice cream: $\frac{1}{3}$ of the amount they make is vanilla, $\frac{1}{6}$ is strawberry and $\frac{1}{12}$ is chocolate. The rest is raspberry ripple. What fraction is raspberry ripple?

7 In Shirley's garden, she grows vegetables in $\frac{2}{5}$ of the area, flowers in $\frac{1}{4}$ of the area and the rest is grass. What fraction of her garden is grass?

8 In a survey about pets, $\frac{3}{8}$ of the people asked said they had a dog, $\frac{1}{3}$ said they had a cat and none had both a dog and a cat.

a What fraction didn't have a dog or a cat?

b If 120 people were asked, how many didn't have a dog or a cat?

9 Kathryn was given a bonus of £500 from her work. She spent $\frac{2}{5}$ of it on some new clothes, $\frac{1}{4}$ on a visit to a restaurant, $\frac{1}{8}$ on some music and the rest she put in her savings account.

a What fraction of her bonus did she spend?

b How much did she put in her savings account?

10 Mixed numbers and improper fractions

Exercise 10A Converting mixed numbers to improper fractions

 1 **a** How many fifths are in 1?   **b** How many fifths are in 4?

  c How many fifths are in $4\frac{2}{5}$?   **d** How many sixths are in 1?

  e How many sixths are in 5?   **f** How many sixths are in $5\frac{1}{6}$?

  g How many tenths are in 3?   **h** How many tenths are in $3\frac{7}{10}$?

2 Convert these mixed numbers to improper fractions.

a $2\frac{2}{5}$	**b** $1\frac{1}{6}$	**c** $3\frac{1}{2}$	**d** $2\frac{1}{4}$	**e** $4\frac{2}{7}$
f $5\frac{1}{3}$	**g** $8\frac{4}{5}$	**h** $6\frac{2}{3}$	**i** $4\frac{1}{8}$	**j** $6\frac{5}{6}$
k $3\frac{4}{5}$	**l** $1\frac{9}{10}$	**m** $7\frac{1}{2}$	**n** $2\frac{3}{7}$	**o** $4\frac{3}{4}$
p $8\frac{2}{3}$	**q** $7\frac{5}{6}$	**r** $9\frac{3}{8}$		

> **Hint** An improper fraction has numerator > denominator, e.g. $\frac{5}{4}$
> A mixed number has a whole number part and a fraction part, e.g. $2\frac{2}{5}$

Exercise 10B Converting improper fractions to mixed numbers

 1 Write each of these improper fractions as a mixed number.

a $\frac{5}{2}$	**b** $\frac{7}{6}$	**c** $\frac{13}{4}$	**d** $\frac{12}{5}$	**e** $\frac{11}{3}$
f $\frac{9}{8}$	**g** $\frac{15}{7}$	**h** $\frac{20}{3}$	**i** $\frac{11}{9}$	**j** $\frac{13}{6}$
k $\frac{24}{5}$	**l** $\frac{25}{8}$	**m** $\frac{16}{9}$	**n** $\frac{15}{11}$	**o** $\frac{19}{15}$
p $\frac{17}{12}$	**q** $\frac{33}{10}$	**r** $\frac{38}{7}$		

 2 Write each of these improper fractions as a mixed number, simplifying your answer where necessary.

a $\frac{18}{8}$	**b** $\frac{18}{4}$	**c** $\frac{16}{10}$	**d** $\frac{10}{6}$	**e** $\frac{21}{9}$
f $\frac{35}{15}$	**g** $\frac{36}{21}$	**h** $\frac{38}{14}$	**i** $\frac{54}{12}$	**j** $\frac{16}{6}$
k $\frac{52}{8}$	**l** $\frac{92}{20}$	**m** $\frac{33}{15}$	**n** $\frac{50}{16}$	**o** $\frac{111}{30}$
p $\frac{66}{9}$	**q** $\frac{115}{25}$	**r** $\frac{21}{12}$		

11 Ratio and proportion

Exercise 11A Ratio and proportion

Example 11.1

For the strip shown:

a work out the proportion of the strip that is shaded. Write your answer as a fraction, a decimal fraction and a percentage

b work out the ratio of the shaded part to the unshaded part.

a Shaded proportion = $\frac{3}{10}$ = 0.3 = 30% — *The shaded proportion is the number of shaded squares divided by the total number of squares.*

b shaded : unshaded

$\qquad$ 3 : 7 — *Write the ratio in the order asked in the question. There are 3 shaded and 7 unshaded squares, so the ratio is 3 : 7. You say this as '3 to 7'.*

1 For each of these strips:

    i work out the proportion of the strip that is shaded. Write your answer as a fraction, a decimal fraction and a percentage

    ii work out the ratio of the shaded part to the unshaded part.

    a

    b

    c

2 The diagrams show groups of different shapes. For each group of shapes, work out:

    i the proportion of the group that are circles. Write your answers as fractions, simplifying where possible

    ii the ratio of circles to squares.

    a   **b**

    c   **d**

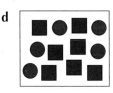

3 Look at the diagram below.

    a What proportion of the squares are grey?

    b What proportion of the squares are white?

    c What is the ratio of grey squares to white squares?

    d If the pattern continued and the diagram was extended to have a total of 48 squares, how many would be grey?

4 In the diagram below, what is the ratio of grey squares to white squares?

5 Purple Dazzle paint is made by mixing 600 ml of blue paint with 400 ml of red paint.

    a What is the total volume of paint?

    b What proportion of the paint is blue? Give your answer as a fraction, a decimal fraction and a percentage.

    c If a batch of 35 litres of paint was mixed, how much red paint would be needed?

6 3 packets of chocolate biscuits cost £4.05. How much would each of the following cost?

    a 1 packet   **b** 4 packets   **c** 8 packets   **d** 12 packets

7 US$3 (3 US dollars) are worth £2.31. How many pounds would each of the following be worth?

    a US$1   **b** US$5   **c** US$12   **d** US$50

8 A recipe for Bolognese sauce to serve 6 people uses 450 g minced steak, 810 g tomatoes, 1 large onion and 3 cloves of garlic.

    a How much of each ingredient would be needed for 12 people?

    b How much of each ingredient would be needed for 5 people?

9 A restaurant bill came to a total of £75 for 4 people. £10.50 of this was for drinks and the rest was for food. What proportion of the bill was spent on food?

10 A plumber earned £350 for fitting a central heating boiler, a job that lasted for 4 hours.

    a What was his hourly rate for this job?

    b How much would he have charged for a job lasting 6 hours at the same rate?

Exercise 11B Simplifying ratios

Example 11.2

Write the ratio 18:12 in its simplest form.

18:12

18 ÷ 6 : 12 ÷ 6 ●———————— Divide both parts of the ratio by their highest common factor (HCF). The HCF of 18 and 12 is 6.

3:2

1 Write each of these ratios in its simplest form.

    a 2:6   **b** 3:9   **c** 12:4   **d** 4:6

    e 15:12   **f** 6:15   **g** 28:49   **h** 54:30

    i 56:80   **j** 45:108   **k** 30:12   **l** 30:18

2 In a bag of 20 counters, there are 4 blue counters, 6 red, 8 green and the rest are yellow.

    a Write down the proportion of each colour as a percentage.

    b Find each of these ratios in its simplest form.

        i blue:green   **ii** red:yellow

        iii blue:red:green   **iv** blue:red:green:yellow

3 A recipe for scones uses 500 g of flour, 30 g of sugar and 75 g of butter. Write these ratios in their simplest form.

    a flour to butter   **b** sugar to butter

    c flour to sugar   **d** sugar to butter to flour

4 Express each of these ratios in its simplest form.

    a 20 cm:35 cm   **b** 500 mm:300 mm   **c** 64 m:24 m

    d 50 mm:75 mm   **e** 450 cm:720 cm   **f** 42 mm:66 mm

    g 40 km:96 km   **h** 105 m:28 m

Exercise 11C Using equivalent ratios

1 Copy and complete these equivalent ratios.

    a 2:3   **b** 5:4   **c** 3:5   **d** 4:5

       6:?   20:?   24:?   ?:35

    e 7:10   **f** 2:5   **g** 2:3:5   **h** 4:1:3

       ?:250   ?:150   ?:9:?   ?:?:120

2 The ratio of milk chocolates to dark chocolates in a box is 3:2. If there are 18 milk chocolates, how many dark chocolates are in the box?

3 Purple Dazzle paint is made by mixing 6 parts of blue paint with 4 parts of red paint.

    a How much red paint would you need if you had the following amounts of blue?

        i 60 ml   **ii** 30 ml   **iii** 15 ml   **iv** 50 ml

    b How much blue paint would you need if you had the following amounts of red?

        i 200 ml   **ii** 100 ml   **iii** 50 ml   **iv** 600 ml

4 A recipe for Bolognese sauce to serve 6 people uses 450 g minced steak, 810 g tomatoes, 1 large onion and 3 cloves of garlic.

    a Write down the ratio of minced steak to tomatoes in its simplest form.

    b What weight of tomatoes would you need if you had 200 g of minced steak?

Exercise 11D Dividing quantities in a given ratio

Example 11.3

The ratio of adults to children in a tennis club is 5:4. If the club has 126 members, how many are adults and how many are children?

$5 + 4 = 9$ ————————(Add the parts of the ratio.)

$126 \div 9 = 14$ ————————(Divide the total by the number of parts to find the 'value' of 1 part.)

$5 \times 14 = 70$ and $4 \times 14 = 56$ ———(Multiply the value of 1 part by each part of the ratio to find how many of each there are.)

There are 70 adults and 56 children.

Check: $70 + 56 = 126$ ✓ ———(Check that your answers add to the original total.)

1 Divide £360 in the following ratios.

    a 2:1   **b** 5:4   **c** 1:3   **d** 5:7   **e** 7:11

2 A lottery win of £2800 is shared between Angus and Dougal in the ratio 5:3. How much does each of them win?

3 In a typical sample of UK honey, the ratio of sugar to water is approximately 4:1. What quantity of sugar and water would be in a 340 g jar?

4 AmberGlow paint is made by mixing yellow paint with red in the ratio 4:3. A particular batch made 35 litres of AmberGlow. How much yellow and red paint was needed?

5 The ratio of female to male MSPs in the Scottish Parliament is approximately 15:28. There are 129 MSPs in total. How many MSPs are female and how many are male?

6 A fertiliser used to feed tomatoes is a mixture of nitrogen, phosphates and potash in the ratio 6:5:9. How much of each type of chemical compound is in a 1.3-litre bottle?

7 SunFresh Fruit drink is made by mixing orange juice, pineapple juice and water in the ratio 3:2:5.

    a What are the proportions of each type of juice in the drink? Give your answers as a percentage.

    b A carton contains 2 litres of SunFresh. How much of this is pineapple juice?

8 An electricity bill for £182 is shared between Grace, Ross and Ella in the ratio 6:5:3. How much does each person pay?

12 Money: Contracts and services

Exercise 12A Finding the best deal

Example 12.1

A washing machine is sold by an online store for £399. A high-street retailer sells the same machine for £450 minus a cash discount of 15%. Which shop offers the better deal and by how much?

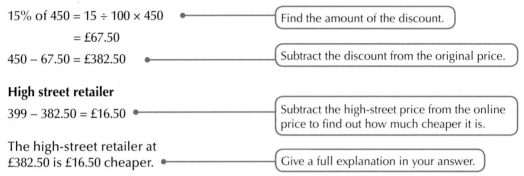

Online store

15% of 450 = 15 ÷ 100 × 450 ———• ⟨ Find the amount of the discount. ⟩

= £67.50

450 − 67.50 = £382.50 ———• ⟨ Subtract the discount from the original price. ⟩

High street retailer

399 − 382.50 = £16.50 ———• ⟨ Subtract the high-street price from the online price to find out how much cheaper it is. ⟩

The high-street retailer at
£382.50 is £16.50 cheaper. ———• ⟨ Give a full explanation in your answer. ⟩

1. A hybrid bike is being sold by an outdoors shop for £550 less a discount of £75 in their sale. The same bike is on offer at a bike shop for £540 minus a 10% discount.

   a Which shop is offering the better deal?

   b How much cheaper is the better deal?

2. A supermarket sells cans of fizzy drink in two different sizes of multipack. A pack of 8 cans costs £3.50 or a pack of 12 cans costs £4.50. Which multipack is cheaper per can? By how much?

3. A small tin of peas contains 250 g and costs 35 p. A large tin of the same peas costs 65 p and contains 454 g. Which tin is the better buy for the price per gram?

4. A supermarket sells chocolate finger biscuits at 60 p for a four-finger biscuit or you can buy a multipack of 8 two-finger biscuits for £1.59. Which of these is cheaper per finger? By how much?

5. A 200 g jar of coffee is normally sold for £7.49, but has been reduced to £6.50 in a promotion. The same brand of coffee is also available in a 100 g jar for £3.85 or a 150 g refill pack for £4.50.

   a Which is the best deal for the price per gram?

   b What is the difference in price per 100 g between the best deal and the most expensive option?

6. Tickets to see Stratus Quire in Inverness cost £32 plus a service charge of £3.20 each from the online agents Ticket Trader. A ticket collection charge of £3.00 is also added to each order. The venue's box office offered the same tickets for £32 plus 10% to cover all fees. Which is the less expensive option for 2 tickets? By how much?

7 Cameron wants to buy 1300 litres of heating oil for his house. He gets quotes from three different companies:

- Oil Deals for 45.26 p per litre plus a 2% credit charge
- BestOil for 43.35 p per litre plus a 5% credit charge
- North Fuel for 47.20 p per litre.

Which one would be his cheapest option?

8 A local car dealer sells a used people carrier for £15 798 with an extra 5% discount for having no trade-in. A similar vehicle is being sold by a national dealership for £15 485 with a special offer of a £450 reduction for buying this week. Which dealer offers the better deal?

9 Kaylah travels to work every day on the bus. She works for 5 days each week for a period of 4 weeks. The bus company offers three different ticket options for her journey:

- a day return ticket costing £5.90
- a weekly ticket costing £16.15
- a 4-week ticket costing £62.

a i Which ticket offers her the best deal?

   ii How much would she save compared with the most expensive option?

b Is it still the best option if she reduces her hours to only working for 3 weeks each month?

10 A phone company offers three different SIM-only plans:

- 500 MB data, 250 minutes and unlimited texts for £5 per month
- 1.5 GB data, 2000 minutes and 1000 texts for £6 per month
- 2 GB data, 1500 minutes and unlimited texts for £10 per month.

Which one would be the best deal if:

a you spend a lot of time talking to friends?

b you want to stream TV to your phone?

c you only send texts?

11 Mr and Mrs Thomas want to upgrade their broadband at home and were comparing different companies' contracts. They narrowed the choice down to the following three companies.

Company	Speed	Monthly cost	Contract length	Setup charge	Extras
A	38 Mb	£32.49	18 months	free	£100 cash back
B	17 Mb	£21	18 months	£7	
C	38 Mb	£25.99	18 months	£9.99	£50 voucher

Which one should they choose for:

a the lowest cost in the first year?

b cheapest high speed for on-demand services?

Exercise 12B Borrowing money

1 A new 55 inch 4K Smart TV costs £955. The retailer offers the option to spread the payments over 52 weeks for £25 per week.

   a What is the total cost of the TV using this option?

   b How much extra does it cost to pay in instalments?

2 A microwave oven costs £320. A buyer can take it away today by paying either the full amount or by paying a deposit of £50 plus 26 weekly payments of £11.50. Which option is the better deal?

3 Alan needs to borrow £2000 to help pay for some building work. Two banks offer him the following deals:

   • Forres Bank offers 1 year loans up to £5000 at an interest rate of 4% p.a. (per annum)

   • Bank of Biggar offers £2000 for 12 monthly payments of £180.

   Which is the better deal?

4 Sarah wants to borrow £400 for a holiday.

   • Her bank offers her a £400 loan for 1 year with an interest rate of 6%.

   • A short-term loan company offers her a 3-month loan with monthly payments of £195.75.

   Work out the total cost of each option. How much does she save by choosing the cheaper option?

5 A hybrid bike is being sold by a bike shop for £550. They offer an option to either pay the full amount today or spread the cost over 24 months for £23.50 per month. How much extra does it cost to pay by instalments?

6 Tony wants to buy a new guitar for £399. He doesn't have the money to buy it outright now, but the shop offers him the option of paying a deposit of £100 plus 9 instalments of £39.90 per month. Alternatively, his father will lend him the money provided he pays back £15 per week for 28 weeks from his part-time job. Which is the cheaper option?

7 Jennifer and Ben want to find a mortgage of £135 000 to buy their first house together. Three different lenders offer these options:

   • lender A: repayment of £445 per month for 30 years

   • lender B: repayment of £520 per month for 25 years

   • lender C: repayment of £835 per month for 15 years.

   They can afford to pay up to £600 per month. Which is the best deal for them?

8 Olivia wants to buy a new car costing £10 999. She has two options to pay for the car:

   • she pays a deposit of £999 followed by 48 monthly payments of £242.38

   • she gets a loan from the bank for the full amount with no deposit and pays 48 monthly payments of £245.17.

   Which option has the lower overall cost?

13 Money: Budgeting

Exercise 13A Income and expenditure

1 Katrina decided to make a note of the money she spent and earned in the last 4 weeks.

Week	Income	Expenditure
1	£76.42	£55.20
2	£125.00	£68.99
3	£65.28	£50.40
4	£85.50	£48.15

    a Calculate her total income and expenditure over this period.

    b How much did she save in this time?

    c How long would it take her to save £250 if she saves at the same rate?

2 Joe is keeping track of his money so he can save for a new bike. The details for one week are shown in the table.

Day	Income	Expenditure
Mon	Pocket money, £20	
Tue		Cinema, £15
Wed		
Thu		
Fri	Paper round, £35	Magazine, £5
Sat	Cut grass, £5	
Sun		Burger, £5

    a Calculate his total income and expenditure for the week.

    b How much did he save in that week?

    c The bike he wants costs £395. If he saves the same amount each week, how many weeks will it take him to save enough money for it?

3 The Robinson family are starting a budget to keep control of their money. They plan to save the difference between the initial and final balance each month. Part of their bank account statement for last month is given below.

Date	Description	Paid in	Paid out	Balance
1-Jun				278.14
2-Jun	Electricity		35.00	
2-Jun	Shopping		98.58	
6-Jun	Council tax		72.00	
11-Jun	Phone contracts		55.00	
14-Jun	Salary payment	1452.00		
15-Jun	Fuel		65.00	
17-Jun	Mortgage		820.00	
22-Jun	Supermarket shopping		192.00	
23-Jun	Credit card refund	35.00		
30-Jun	Cash point		40.00	

    a Copy and complete the balance column for the statement.

    b How much money did the Robinsons save in June?

    c They are saving for a family holiday costing £1200. How long will it take them at the same rate of saving?

4 John's income and expenditure for one week in April are shown below.

Date	Description	Paid in	Paid out	Balance
2-Apr				185.00
3-Apr	Rent		112.50	72.50
3-Apr	Shopping		52.00	20.50
4-Apr	Electricity		5.00	15.50
5-Apr	Phone contract		6.00	9.50
6-Apr	Gym membership		20.00	−10.50
7-Apr	Wage	328.00		317.50
7-Apr	Broadband		15.00	302.50
8-Apr	Credit card		140.00	162.50

a Calculate John's total income and expenditure for this week.

b Did he save any money during this week?

c What expenses could he cut back on to save some money next month?

5 April and Ali are given £40 to go to a football match. The return bus fare into town is £1.25 each, match tickets cost £12 each and they can buy a pie and hot drink each in the ground for £6.50.

a Do they have enough left for a programme costing £3? Show your working.

b What could they cut back on to save enough for a programme?

6 The Hassan family want to build a 2 m by 3 m rectangular deck at the back of their house. Their budget is £200. They have worked out that they will need the following materials:

- 18 decking boards at £22.50 for a pack of 5

- 12 decking joists at £6 each

- 1 box of screws at £7.32

- 1 tin of decking stain at £25.

Can they build their deck within the £200 budget? Show your calculations.

7 Peter is planning a trip to the Wildlife Park with a friend and their 2 children. The 2 adults have a budget of £60 each for the day.

a Use the information below to work out the cheapest cost of their trip.

- *Travel:* Car fuel, £35 *or* Train ticket, adults £16, children go free

- *Park entry:* Adults £15.90, children £12

- *Food:* Park café lunch deal, £6 each *or* Bring own sandwiches, £3.50 each

- *Drinks:* Coffee, £2.50 and soft drink, £1.25 *or* Bring flask and drinks, £2.50

b Do they have any money left to spend in the souvenir shop? If yes, how much?

c Calculate the most expensive overall cost for the trip. Is it within the budget?

8 Katie and Tom want to order a meal from their local Chinese takeaway.

Katie wants to order spicy chicken wings at £5.00, Thai chilli chicken for £5.80 and fried rice for £2.20

Tom wants to order spring rolls for £3.20, beef in black bean sauce for £5.50 and plain noodles for £3.20.

The restaurant also offers a meal deal for a minimum of two people that includes any starter, main course, side dish and a soft drink for £10.80 each.

a Is it cheaper for them to order their dishes individually or to choose the meal deal?

b How much could they save using the cheaper option?

Exercise 13B Exchange rates

Use the following exchange rates for the questions in this exercise:

£1 = €1.12 (euro) £1 = US$1.29 (US dollars) £1 = AU$1.64 (Australian dollars)

£1 = JPY¥145.27 (Japanese yen) £1 = CNY¥8.77 (Chinese yuan)

Example 13.1

Convert the following:

a £50 to US dollars **b** AU$395 to UK pounds.

a 50 × 1.29 = US$64.50 — To convert from UK pounds to another currency, multiply by the exchange rate.

b 395 ÷ 1.64 = 240.85365 — To convert from another currency to UK pounds, divide by the exchange rate.

= £240.85 — Round your answer down to the nearest penny. Currencies should always be rounded down, as this is what financial institutions do.

1 Change the following to the currency shown.

a £200 to Japanese yen (¥)

b £1000 to euro (€)

c £473 to Chinese yuan

2 Convert the following amounts into UK pounds. Round your answers to the nearest penny.

a €100 **b** US$100 **c** AU$100 **d** JPY¥100 **e** CNY¥100

f AU$350 **g** CNY¥795 **h** US$58 **i** JPY¥52 000 **j** €125

3 Kate wants to give AU$150 to her grandson in Australia for his birthday. How much will it cost her in pounds?

4 A return journey from London to Brussels on the Eurostar costs £44. The same journey from Brussels to London costs €52.64. Which journey is cheaper?

5 Alan changed £500 into US dollars for his holiday. He spent US$520 while he was away and changed the rest back into pounds when he got back. How much, to the nearest penny, did he bring back in pounds?

6 Aidan spends his summer picking grapes in Spain. He converts €268.80 of his earnings into pounds sterling and takes the money with him on a trip back to the UK.

How much does he take with him?

7 Lesley wants to move to a Mediterranean resort, so she sells her house in Glasgow for £285 000.

Does she make enough money to buy a house in Italy that costs €310 000?

8 Andrew wants to import a sports car from the USA that costs $26 500 in Florida. Can he afford to buy the car on his budget of £20 000?

9 The Blacks are going on a trip to China and want to change £450 into Chinese yuan for spending money. Two travel agents offer the following exchange rates:

- Best Travel: £1 = CNY¥8.77

- China First: £1 = CNY¥8.88 plus 2% commission

Which travel agent offers the better deal?

> **Hint** Remember: the 2% commission is subtracted from the initial amount.

10 Helen lives in Dundee. She is going to a theme park in France with her family. Their party consists of 2 adults and 3 children.

She has two ways of buying entry tickets.

- Her local travel agent can sell her entry tickets for £56 each for adults and £51 each for children.

- An agent in Paris sells all tickets for €60 each.

Should she buy their tickets in Dundee or in Paris?

11 David buys a watch on holiday in Japan for JPY¥14 500. When he returns home, he sees the same watch for sale in his local jewellers for £120. Did he get a good deal buying the watch in Japan?

14 Speed, distance and time

Exercise 14A Time intervals

1 Calculate the length of time from:

   a 6:30 pm to 9:50 pm   **b** 7:45 am to 1:10 pm   **c** 10:30 pm to 7:20 am

   d 2:50 pm to 6:25 pm   **e** 1:32 am to 12:15 pm   **f** 9:48 pm to 11:16 am

2 Calculate the time interval from:

   a 08:20 to 12:45   **b** 13:20 to 18:08   **c** 23:12 to 05:30

   d 11:42 to 23:23   **e** 21:30 to 15:03   **f** 00:36 to 15:18

3 An extract from the train timetable between Inverness and Aberdeen is shown below.

Inverness	1427	1529	1714	1813
Forres	1453	1557	1741	1839
Huntly	1545	1650	1847	1942
Aberdeen	1641	1746	1940	2035

   a How long does the journey from Inverness to Aberdeen take on the 1427 train?

   b How long does the 1714 train take to travel from Forres to Huntly?

   c Which train takes the longest to travel from Inverness to Aberdeen?

4 The table shows some of the start times and lengths for three films in the cinema.

Film	Start time		
Blade Runner 2049 (2 hours 44 min)	12:30	16:00	19:30
Flatliners (1 hour 50 min)	17:30	20:00	
The Lego Ninjago Movie	10:00	12:30	15:00

   a When does the 4 pm showing of *Blade Runner 2049* finish?

   b The 12:30 showing of *The Lego Ninjago Movie* finishes at 14:11. How long does it last?

   c How much longer is *Blade Runner 2049* than *Flatliners*?

5 Clare took a trip by car from Inverness to Glasgow. It took 2 hours and 28 minutes to get to Perth, where she stopped for 45 minutes. She then took a further 1 hour and 10 minutes to reach Glasgow. If she left Inverness at 8:45 am, when did she get to Glasgow?

6 Alistair took part in a 95 mile cross-country endurance race. He started at 7:30 pm and finished at 5:18 pm the next day. How long did he take to complete the course?

Exercise 14B Calculating speed

1 Calculate the average speed of these journeys.

   a 150 miles in 3 hours   **b** 325 km in 5 hours   **c** 220 m in 40 s   **d** 73 miles in 4 hours

> **Hint** Use the formula $\text{speed} = \dfrac{\text{distance}}{\text{time}}$ or $s = \dfrac{d}{t}$
>
> Remember to include the units in your answer.

2 A motorbike travels 425 km in 5 hours. Calculate the average speed.

3 Usain Bolt's record for the 100 m is 9.58 seconds. How fast was this in metres per second? Round your answer to 1 decimal place.

4 The distance from Glasgow to Stonehaven is 130 miles. A single journey between them on the train takes 3 hours. Calculate the average speed of the train, rounding your answer to 1 decimal place.

5 An HGV driver is required to keep to a maximum average speed limit of 50 mph on the A9. The journey from Perth to Inverness is 112 miles and a MegaPost courier completes it in 2 and a half hours. Did the driver stay below the 50 mph speed limit?

Exercise 14C Calculating distance

1 Calculate the distance travelled on these journeys.

    a 4 hours at 45 mph   **b** 9 hours at 70 km/h   **c** 3.5 s at 15 m/s   **d** 82.5 km/h for 7 hours

> **Hint** Use the formula distance = speed × time or $d = s \times t$
> Remember to include the units in your answer.

2 A train travels at a speed of 150 km/h for 5 hours. What distance does it travel in this time?

3 Annabelle cycles at an average speed of 4 mph. How far does she travel in 2 hours and 30 minutes?

4 The average speed of a garden snail is 0.03 mph. How far could it travel in 1 week if it did not stop?

5 Alice walked at an average speed of 6 km/h for 2 hours and 15 minutes. Billy cycled for half an hour at an average speed of 30 km/h. Who travelled further and by how much?

Exercise 14D Calculating time

1 Calculate the time taken to complete these journeys.

    a 510 km at 85 km/h   **b** 270 miles at 60 mph   **c** 100 m at 12.5 m/s   **d** 8.75 km at 2.5 km/h

> **Hint** Use the formula time = $\dfrac{\text{distance}}{\text{speed}}$ or $t = \dfrac{d}{s}$
> Remember to include units in your answer.

2 How long does it take to travel 225 miles at an average speed of 45 mph?

3 An ostrich can run at an average speed of 40 mph. How long would it take to run 100 miles if it could keep running at the same average speed?

4 A ball rolls downhill at an average speed of 2.5 m/s. How long does it take to roll 100 m downhill?

5 Chris cycled at an average speed of 12.5 km/h for 25 km. Paula ran at an average speed of 12 km/h for 18 km. Who took longer to complete their race?

Exercise 14E Mixed calculations

1 A truck drove on the motorway at an average speed of 85 km/h. What distance did it travel in 3 hours and 45 minutes?

2 A tour bus travelled a distance of 192 km at an average speed of 40 km/h. How long did it take to travel this distance? Give your answer in hours and minutes.

3 Daniel drove from his house to Blackpool, a distance of 196 miles. It took him 3 hours and 30 minutes. What was his average speed?

4 An arrow fired from an archery bow takes 1.26 s to travel 70 metres to the target. What is its average speed? Round your answer to 1 decimal place.

5 The International Space Station orbits the Earth at a speed of approximately 5 miles per second.

   a How far does it travel in 50 minutes?

   b The distance it travels in one orbit of the Earth is approximately 276 000 miles. How many minutes does it take to complete one orbit?

Exercise 14F Distance–time graphs

1 This graph shows a car journey in three stages.

   a Calculate the average speed of the car during:

      i the first 2 hours   **ii** the third hour.

   b What was the car doing in the fourth hour? Calculate its speed during this part of the journey.

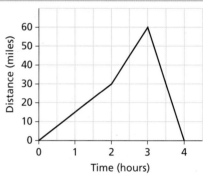

2 This graph shows the three stages of Alana's journey from home to school.

   a What speed was she walking at during the first 5 minutes?

   b What was she doing in the next 5 minutes?

   c What speed was she doing in the final stage of her journey?

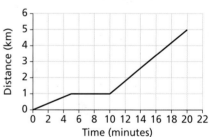

3 The tables below show car journeys, where all distances are the distance from home. Draw a distance–time graph for each journey. Describe the journeys for each graph, including its speed for each part of the journey, any parts where it stopped and for how long.

a

Time (hours)	0	1	2	3	4	5
Distance (miles)	0	10	20	20	50	50

b

Time (hours)	0	1	2	3	4	5
Distance (miles)	60	60	40	20	10	0

c

Time (hours)	0	1	2	3	4	5
Distance (km)	0	40	40	60	60	0

4 Claire and Dave live 70 km away from each other. The graph shows the journeys they each made as they decided to visit each other's towns one day.

   a Who left home first?

   b If the first journey started at 10:00 am, at what time did they pass each other on the road?

   c Whose average speed was faster?

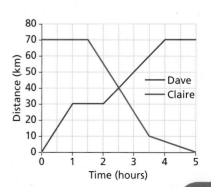

15 Perimeter, area and volume

Exercise 15A Perimeter and area of rectangles 🖩

1 For each of the following rectangles, find:

   i the perimeter   **ii** the area

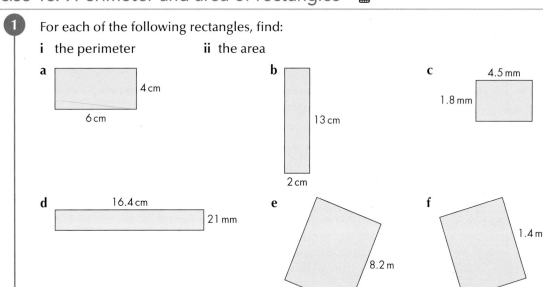

a — 6 cm, 4 cm
b — 13 cm, 2 cm
c — 4.5 mm, 1.8 mm
d — 16.4 cm, 21 mm
e — 580 cm, 8.2 m
f — 1.4 m, 90 cm

> **Hint** Remember to check both measurements use the same unit before calculating.

2 An A4 sheet of paper measures 21.0 cm × 29.7 cm.

Find:

  a its perimeter   **b** its area

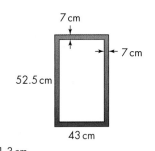

A4 Pad — 29.7 cm, 21.0 cm

3 The outside of a picture frame measures 52.5 cm × 43 cm.

The picture frame has a border of 7 cm.

Calculate the area of the picture inside the frame.

7 cm, 7 cm, 52.5 cm, 43 cm

4 A 30 cm ruler measures 31.3 cm × 42 mm.

Calculate the area it covers on your desk.

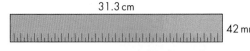

31.3 cm, 42 mm

5 Mrs Thomson's flower garden measures 12.8 m × 7.2 m.

It has a 1 m flower border surrounding a rectangular area of grass.

  a Calculate the area of the grass.

  b A carton of grass feed costing £5.99 will treat up to 30 m²
    of grass. How much will it cost Mrs Thomson to feed
    her grass?

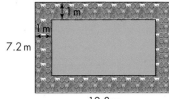

1 m, 1 m, 7.2 m, 12.8 m

1 Calculate the area of each triangle.

a
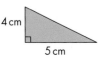
4 cm
5 cm

b

5 m
3 m

c

3.6 m
2 m

d
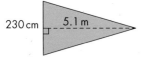
230 cm
5.1 m

e
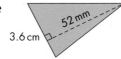
52 mm
3.6 cm

f
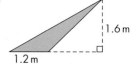
1.6 m
1.2 m

> **Hint** The area of a triangle is given by $A = \frac{1}{2}bh$ or $A = \frac{bh}{2}$
>
> where b is the length of the base and h is the height.
> These are always at right angles to each other.

2 A set-square is shown in the diagram.
Find its area.

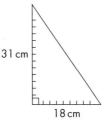
31 cm
18 cm

3 The diagram shows the roof support inside a building.
Calculate the area under the roof.

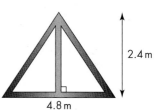
2.4 m
4.8 m

4 A park flower bed is in the shape of a triangle, as shown.
Calculate the area of the flower bed.

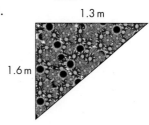
1.3 m
1.6 m

5 The end of this take-away sandwich pack is triangular.
Calculate its area.

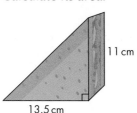
11 cm
13.5 cm

Exercise 15C Area of quadrilaterals

> **Hint** You will need these formulae:
>
> | Parallelogram | Trapezium | Rhombus and kite |
> |---|---|---|
> | 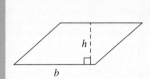 | 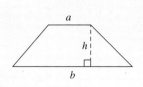 | 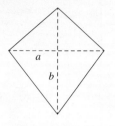 |
> | $A = bh$ | $A = \frac{1}{2}(a + b)h$ | $A = \frac{1}{2}ab$ |

1 Calculate the area of these parallelograms.

a

b

c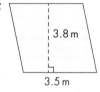

2 Calculate the area of these trapeziums.

a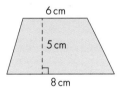

b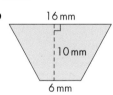

c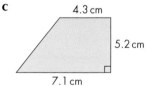

3 Calculate the area of these quadrilaterals.

a

b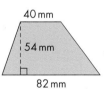

c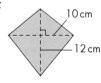

d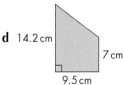

e

f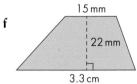

4 The diagram shows the end of a lean-to shed.
Calculate its area.

Exercise 15D Volume of a cuboid 🖩

1. Calculate the volume of these cuboids.

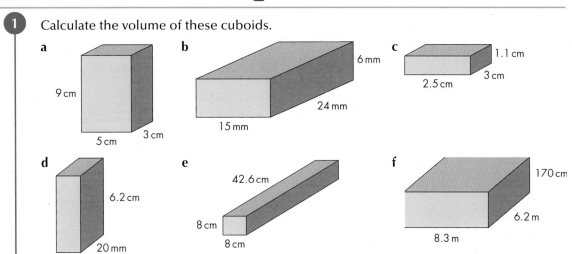

a 9 cm, 5 cm, 3 cm

b 6 mm, 24 mm, 15 mm

c 1.1 cm, 3 cm, 2.5 cm

d 6.2 cm, 20 mm, 8 mm

e 42.6 cm, 8 cm, 8 cm

f 170 cm, 6.2 m, 8.3 m

2. Find the capacity of these containers in litres.

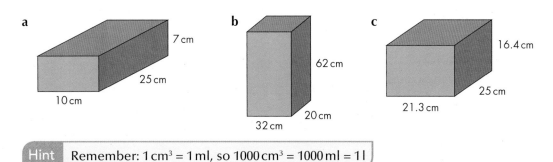

a 7 cm, 25 cm, 10 cm

b 62 cm, 20 cm, 32 cm

c 16.4 cm, 25 cm, 21.3 cm

> **Hint** Remember: $1\,cm^3 = 1\,ml$, so $1000\,cm^3 = 1000\,ml = 1\,l$

3. A length of construction timber is shown in the diagram.
   Calculate its volume.

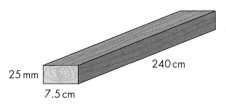

240 cm, 25 mm, 7.5 cm

4. A guitar amplifier has dimensions of 59 cm by 26 cm by 51 cm, as shown.

   a Calculate its volume.

   b Find its capacity, to the nearest litre.

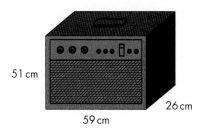

51 cm, 59 cm, 26 cm

5. An apple juice carton measures 5 cm by 4 cm by 11 cm. How many can be packed into a box measuring 60 cm by 52 cm by 56 cm?

Exercise 15E Metric units for area and volume

1 Express each area in the units given in square brackets.

   a 3 m² [cm²]   **b** 16 cm² [mm²]   **c** 2400 mm² [cm²]

   d 780 000 cm² [m²]   **e** 1.4 cm² [mm²]   **f** 35 000 cm² [m²]

2 Express each volume in the units given in square brackets.

   a 8 cm³ [mm³]   **b** 2.1 m³ [cm³]   **c** 4.5 cm³ [mm³]

   d 0.42 m³ [cm³]   **e** 1 200 000 cm³ [m³]   **f** 28 000 mm³ [cm³]

3 Express each volume as a capacity in litres.

   a 25 000 cm³   **b** 8.6 m³   **c** 1320 cm³

   d 530 cm³   **e** 0.57 m³   **f** 25 cm³

4 Express each capacity in the units given in square brackets

   a 580 ml [cl]   **b** 1.67 litres [ml]   **c** 640 ml [litres]

   d 7.9 litres [cl]   **e** 42 cl [ml]

> **Hint**   100 cl = 1 l   cl = centilitre
>   1000 ml = 1 l   ml = millilitre

5 Which solar panel has the larger area: a square measuring 0.8 m by 0.8 m or a rectangle measuring 85 cm by 750 mm?

6 What is the least number of whole sheets of A4 paper, measuring 21 cm by 29.7 cm, it would take to completely cover a square area measuring 1 m by 1 m?

> **Hint**   Sketch a diagram.

7 How many juice cartons measuring 5 cm by 4 cm by 11 cm can you fill from a 5-litre tank?

8 An oil tank in the shape of a cuboid measures 86 cm by 86 cm by 180 cm.

   How many litres of oil can the tank hold? Round your answer to the nearest 100 litres.

16 Compound shapes and objects

Exercise 16A Perimeter and area of compound shapes

1 For each compound shape calculate:

  i the perimeter   **ii** the area.

a
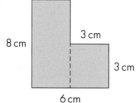

b
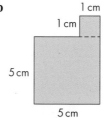

c
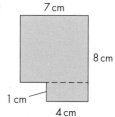

d
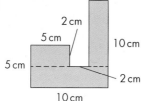

e
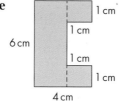

f
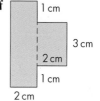

2 Calculate the areas of these compound shapes.

a
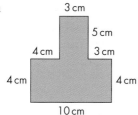

b
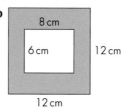

c
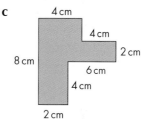

d
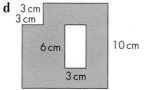

e
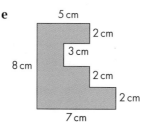

f
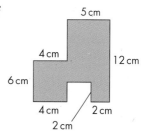

3 A kitchen worktop is shown in the diagram.

Calculate its area.

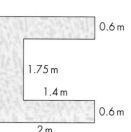

4 A tablet computer measures 20 cm by 13 cm as shown.

There is a 1 cm border surrounding the screen. Calculate the area of the screen.

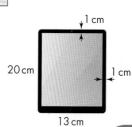

5 Scott is pricing a new carpet for his dining room, which is shown in the diagram.

The carpet he wants costs £21.99 per square metre.

Calculate the cost of the carpet.

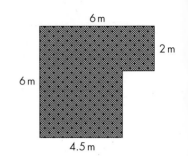

Exercise 16B Compound shapes with triangles

1 Calculate the area of these compound shapes.

a

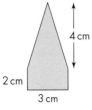

b

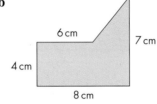

c

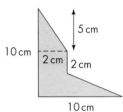

d

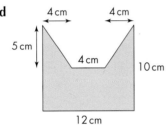

e

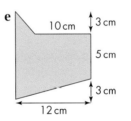

f

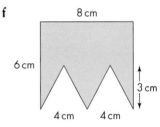

2 A chemical company's logo is shown in the diagram.

Calculate its area.

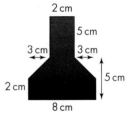

3 A template for drawing around is shown in the diagram.

Calculate the area of paper it covers.

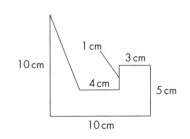

4 The diagram shows a toy shield.

Calculate its area.

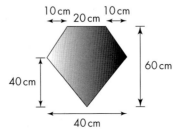

5 Janette wants to paint the end of an outbuilding, which is shown in the diagram. There are two identical windows in the wall.

A tin of paint costs £18.91 and will cover 30 m².

Calculate the cost of applying one coat of paint.

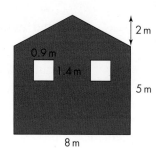

Exercise 16C Volume of compound objects

1 Calculate the volume of these 3D objects.

a

b

c

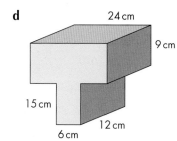 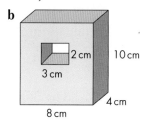 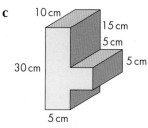

d

e

f

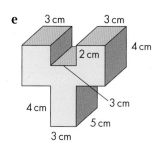 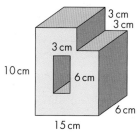

2 A tourist centre wants to reproduce an ancient monument using concrete.

Calculate the volume of concrete they will need for the job.

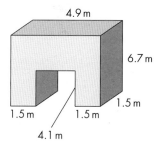

  3 A wooden garden table consists of a flat top surface and a central leg, as shown in the diagram. An extra 40 cm of the leg is buried in the ground to support the table.

Calculate the volume of wood used to make the table.

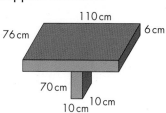

17 Famous mathematicians and mathematical topics

Exercise 17A Famous mathematicians and mathematical topics

Use your research skills to answer these questions about some famous mathematicians and mathematical topics.

1 *Archimedes*

   a What did he discover one day while having a bath and thinking about how to tell if the king's new crown was made of 24-carat gold or not?

   b What did he discover about the relationship between a sphere and a cylinder with the same diameter and height?

   c What method did he use to find the area of a circle and an approximate value for π?

2 *Isaac Newton*

   a What major branch of maths did he discover around the same time as Gottfried Leibniz?

   b What was he studying when he found out about gravity?

   c Why was he interested in gold?

3 *Carl Friedrich Gauss*

   a How did he outwit his teacher at the age of 7?

   b What did he discover how to construct using only a ruler and pair of compasses?

   c What result about prime numbers did this lead to?

4 π

   a What is π?

   b What approximations have been used over the centuries?

   c How many decimal places are currently known?

5 *The golden ratio*

   a What is the golden ratio?

   b What does it have to do with the Fibonacci sequence?

   c Why is it beautiful?

6 *Fractals*

   a When were fractals first discovered and by whom?

   b What is Koch's snowflake?

   c Where would you find fractals in the supermarket? Where else are they used?

18 Sequences

Exercise 18A Sequences and rules

1 Use the given first term and term-to-term rule to find the first 5 terms of these sequences.

   a Start at 2, add 5   **b** Start at 1, add 6   **c** Start at 2, multiply by 3

   d Start at 3, multiply by 5   **e** Start at 20, subtract 4   **f** Start at 36, subtract 9

2 Find the next 2 terms in these sequences and describe the term-to-term rule you used.

   a 1, 4, 7, 10, …   **b** 2, 6, 10, 14, …   **c** 1, 3, 9, 27, …

   d 5, 10, 20, 40, …   **e** 3, 12, 48, 192, …   **f** −12, −8, −4, 0, …

3 Find the missing terms in these sequences and describe the term-to-term rule you used.

   a 100, 88, 76, 64, …, …   **b** 32, 24, 16, 8, …, …   **c** 12, 7, 2, −3, …, …

   d 1.5, 4, 6.5, 9, …, …   **e** 48, 24, 12, 6, …, …   **f** 1.6, 1.3, 1, 0.7, …, …

   g 2150, 215, 21.5, 2.15, …, …   **h** 4, 2, 1, $\frac{1}{2}$, $\frac{1}{4}$, …, …   **i** 2, 6, …, …, 18

   j 5, 11, …, …, 29   **k** 41, 32, …, …, 5   **l** 2, 8, …, …, 512

4 For each of these sequences, find the fifth and the 50th terms.

   a 5, 9, 13, 17, …   **b** 2, 8, 14, 20, …   **c** 3, 8, 13, 18, …

   d 6, 14, 22, 30, …   **e** 4, 13, 22, 31, …   **f** 9, 19, 29, 39, …

   g 15, 30, 45, 60, …   **h** 12, 23, 34, 45, …

> **Hint** To find the 50th term, add 49 times the difference to the first term.

5 Find the 100th term in the sequence with this term-to-term rule: start at 7, add 8.

6 Find the 80th term in the sequence with this term-to-term rule: start at 14, add 12.

Exercise 18B The nth term

1 In each of the sequences below, the formula for the nth term is given.

Find:

i the first 5 terms

ii the 100th term.

   a $2n$ **b** $6n$ **c** $n + 4$ **d** $n - 4$ **e** $2n + 5$

   f $3n - 2$ **g** $6n - 4$ **h** $\frac{1}{2}n + 3$ **i** $\frac{1}{3}n - \frac{1}{6}$

2 For each of these sequences:

  i find the formula for the *n*th term

  ii use the *n*th term to find the 20th term.

  a 3, 6, 9, 12, 15, …   **b** 5, 6, 7, 8, 9, …   **c** 7, 8, 9, 10, 11, …

  d 15, 30, 45, 60, 75, …   **e** 20, 40, 60, 80, 100, …   **f** 9, 10, 11, 12, 13, …

  g −1, 0, 1, 2, 3, …   **h** $\frac{1}{2}$, 1, $1\frac{1}{2}$, 2, $2\frac{1}{2}$, …

3 For each of these sequences:

  i find the formula for the *n*th term

  ii use the *n*th term to find the 50th term.

  a 7, 9, 11, 13, 15, …   **b** 2, 6, 10, 14, 18, …   **c** 4, 7, 10, 13, 16, …

  d 3, 11, 19, 27, 35, …   **e** 2, 5, 8, 11, 14, …   **f** 9, 15, 21, 27, 33, …

  g 0, 8, 16, 24, 32, …   **h** 2, 14, 26, 38, 50, …

4 For each of these patterns of matchsticks, find:

  i the formula for the *n*th term of the sequence

  ii the number of matchsticks in the 60th term.

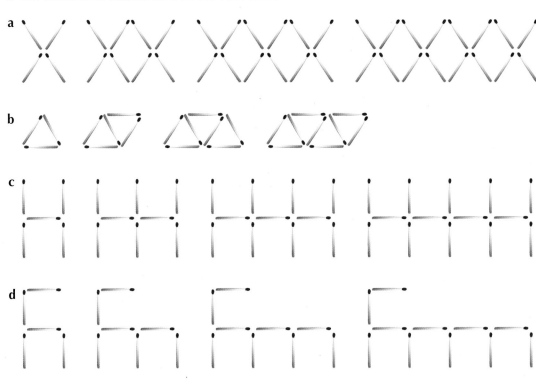

19 Simplifying and evaluating expressions

Exercise 19A Simplifying expressions

Example 19.1

Simplify these expressions:

a $5a \times 2b$ **b** $16p \div 8$

a $5a \times 2b = 5 \times 2 \times a \times b$ — Multiply the numbers and letters separately.

$\quad = 10ab$ — Write the answer without any multiplication signs.

b $16p \div 8 = \dfrac{^2\cancel{16}p}{\cancel{8}_1}$ — Write the expression as a fraction, then divide 16 by 8 to simplify the numerator.

$\quad = 2p$

1 Simplify these expressions.

  a $n + n + n$ **b** $p + p$ **c** $k + k + k + k + k$ **d** $r + r + r + r$

  e $j + j + j + j + j$ **f** $s + s$ **g** $c + c + c + c + c + c$ **h** $i + i + i$

2 Write these expressions using algebraic notation.

  a $4 \times t$ **b** $8 \times r$ **c** $2 \times w$ **d** $e \times 7$

  e $c \times d$ **f** $j \times k$ **g** $t \div 3$ **h** $9 \div x$

  i $k \times k$ **j** $h \times h$ **k** $a \div b$ **l** $3u \div v$

3 Simplify these expressions.

  a $3f \times g$ **b** $p \times 6q$ **c** $5m \times 2n$ **d** $3e \times 4p$

  e $8a \div 2$ **f** $10j \div 5$ **g** $24x \div 3$ **h** $12s \div 8$

  i $25k \div 10$ **j** $x \times y \times z$ **k** $5f \times g \times 3h$ **l** $7r \times 2s \times 3t$

4 Simplify the following expressions.

  a $4u + 3u$ **b** $6f - 2f$ **c** $5g + 4g - g$ **d** $7c - 4c + 5c$

  e $9a - 6a - 5a$ **f** $5j + 3j - 8j$ **g** $s + 4s - 2s$ **h** $4 \times 3r + 5r$

  i $8c \div 2 + 3c$ **j** $12i \times 2j \div 4$

Example 19.2

Simplify the expression $5a + 2b - 3a + b + a$

$5a + 2b - 3a + b + a$ — Write out the expression.

$= 5a - 3a + a + 2b + b$ — Rewrite, collecting like terms together. Each term keeps the sign in front of it.

$= 3a + 3b$ — Combine like terms to get the expression in its simplest form.

Exercise 19B Collecting like terms

1   Simplify these expressions.

   a $5c + 2 + 3c$ **b** $6b + 4 - b$ **c** $7w + 2w + 9$ **d** $8 + 2p + 5p$

   e $5y - 3y - 3$ **f** $12t + 8 - 8t$ **g** $15r - 9 - r$ **h** $8u + 5u - 10$

   i $11e - 4e - 3$ **j** $4g + 7 - 3g$

2   Simplify these expressions.

   a $3h + 2p + 5h + 2p$ **b** $5j + 2k + 3j + 6k$ **c** $12b + 5c - 8b + c$

   d $9s + 7t - 4s - 4t$ **e** $5g - 3b - 2g + 5b$ **f** $8t - 5v + 2t - v$

   g $4a + 6y - 3a - y$ **h** $7x - 5y + 5x - 4y$ **i** $6j - 2k - 5j + 3k$

3   Simplify these expressions.

   a $4p^2 + p^2$ **b** $7a^2 + 3a^2$ **c** $5w^2 - w^2$

   d $6i^2 - 4i^2$ **e** $4r^2 + 2r^2$ **f** $11r^2 - 5r^2$

   g $5k^2 + 2k^2 - 6k^2$ **h** $2t^2 - 4t^2 + 5t^2$

4   Simplify these expressions.

   a $3ab + 2ab$ **b** $7pq - 5pq$ **c** $8xy - 3xy + xy$

   d $5gh - 4gh - 3gh$ **e** $4st + 3st + 2ts$ **f** $7mn - 2nm - mn$

   g $9xy - 3yx - 6yx$ **h** $5pk - 8kp + 4kp$

5   Simplify these expressions.

   a $5a + 6 + 3a + 5$ **b** $7u + 3v - 2u - v$ **c** $w + 7x - 4x + 2w$

   d $3q - 8t - 3q + 8t$ **e** $3y - 5z + 3z + 2y$ **f** $8e + 2e + 6 - 10e$

   g $9i - 5j + i - j$ **h** $9 + 6h + 6 - 5h$ **i** $3y^2 + 2y - y^2 - 5y$

   j $4bc + 3cd - cd - 2bc$ **k** $2k - 1 + 3k^2 - 5k - 2k^2$ **l** $5r^2 - 4r - 7r^2 + 4 + r - 3$

Exercise 19C Substituting into expressions

Example 19.3

Find the value of the expression $3b + ab$, given $a = 4$ and $b = 7$.

$3b + ab = 3 \times 7 + 4 \times 7$ ⟨ Replace each a and b with the values given, a with 4 and b with 7. ⟩

         $= 21 + 28$ ⟨ Use the correct order of operations to work out the answer. ⟩

         $= 49$

1   Find the value of each expression for these values of k.

   i $k = 3$ **ii** $k = 1$ **iii** $k = 15$ **iv** $k = -2$

   a $k + 6$ **b** $k - 2$ **c** $5k$ **d** $4k + 1$

   e $3k + 2$ **f** $2k + 3$ **g** $5 + 2k$ **h** $6 - k$

2   Find the value of each expression, given $p = 2$ and $q = 5$.

   a $p + q$ **b** $q - p$ **c** $p - q$ **d** $2p + q$

   e $4p + 3q$ **f** $6p - 2q$ **g** $2q - 3p$ **h** $5p - 3q$

3 Evaluate each expression, given $x = 3$, $y = 7$ and $z = -2$.

a $x + y + z$ **b** $2x + 3y - z$ **c** xy **d** yz

e xyz **f** $yx + zx$ **g** y^2 **h** $4x^2$

i $(4x)^2$ **j** $3x^2 - 2y$ **k** $2xy + z^2$ **l** $6(5x - 9)$

Exercise 19D Substituting into formulae

1 The formula to find the power P in an electrical circuit is $P = IV$, where I is the current and V is the voltage. Find P when:

a $I = 3$, $V = 9$ **b** $I = 2.5$, $V = 5$ **c** $I = 0.8$, $V = 12$

2 The perimeter P of a rectangle is given by the formula $P = 2l + 2b$, where l is its length and b is its breadth. Find the perimeter of rectangles with these dimensions.

a $l = 6$ cm, $b = 4$ cm   **b** $l = 12$ cm, $b = 2$ cm   **c** $l = 3.5$ cm, $b = 6.1$ cm

3 Newton's second law of motion can be written as $F = ma$, where F is force, m is mass and a is acceleration. Find the value of F when:

a $m = 25$, $a = 3$ **b** $m = 6$, $a = 25$ **c** $m = 7.5$, $a = 44$ **d** $m = 35$, $a = 9.8$

4 The formula to find the velocity v of a particle moving in a straight line is $v = u + at$. Find v when:

a $u = 3$, $a = 5$, $t = 2$ **b** $u = 0$, $a = 15$, $t = 5$ **c** $u = 2.4$, $a = 9.8$, $t = 3$

5 **a** The formula to find the **exterior** angle e of a regular polygon is $e = \dfrac{360}{n}$, where n is the number of sides. Find e when:

     i $n = 4$ **ii** $n = 6$ **iii** $n = 8$ **iv** $n = 15$

     b Once you know the exterior angle of a regular polygon, the **interior** angle i can be found using the formula $i = 180 - e$. Calculate the interior angle of each polygon in part **a**.

6 If $T = \dfrac{mn}{r^2}$, calculate T when:

a $m = 12$, $n = 3$, $r = 3$ **b** $m = 10$, $n = 14$, $r = 4$ **c** $m = 8$, $n = 4.2$, $r = 0.5$

7 The formula to convert temperatures from degrees Fahrenheit F to degrees Celsius C is $C = \dfrac{5F - 160}{9}$. Use it to convert these temperatures from Fahrenheit to Celsius.

a $59\,°F$ **b** $32\,°F$ **c** $23\,°F$ **d** $98.6\,°F$

8 The formula $D = b^2 - 4ac$ is used to find a quantity called the discriminant of a quadratic equation, D. Find the value of D when:

a $a = 1$, $b = 8$, $c = 2$ **b** $a = 1$, $b = 6$, $c = 9$ **c** $a = 2$, $b = 4$, $c = 4$

9 The formula to calculate the geometric mean of two numbers, a and b, is geometric mean $= \sqrt{ab}$. Find the geometric mean of these sets of numbers.

a $a = 2$, $b = 8$ **b** $a = 3$, $b = 27$ **c** $a = 6$, $b = 6$ **d** $a = 4$, $b = 6$

20 Solving equations

Exercise 20A Single-step equations

1 Solve these equations.

a $p + 4 = 12$	**b** $x + 2 = 9$	**c** $r + 7 = 8$	**d** $d + 3 = 10$
e $8 + x = 14$	**f** $13 + m = 28$	**g** $22 = q + 10$	**h** $31 = w + 7$
i $y - 6 = 5$	**j** $t - 2 = 7$	**k** $z - 3 = 8$	**l** $x - 13 = 7$
m $8 - b = 5$	**n** $24 - y = 19$	**o** $12 = f - 4$	**p** $42 = x - 25$

2 Solve these equations.

a $4a = 12$	**b** $8r = 32$	**c** $2k = 16$	**d** $5g = 65$
e $7x = 56$	**f** $9k = 81$	**g** $42 = 7y$	**h** $36 = 9p$
i $\frac{y}{4} = 6$	**j** $\frac{w}{2} = 3$	**k** $\frac{p}{5} = 9$	**l** $\frac{x}{8} = 6$
m $\frac{t}{4} = 1$	**n** $\frac{z}{7} = 0$	**o** $15 = \frac{x}{2}$	**p** $\frac{s}{2} = 12$

3 Solve these equations.

a $y - 2 = 4$	**b** $m + 3 = 12$	**c** $6w = 42$	**d** $t + 7 = 13$
e $\frac{a}{4} = 11$	**f** $u - 3 = 0$	**g** $22 = 2p$	**h** $k + 9 = 13$
i $b - 5 = 0$	**j** $12i = 36$	**k** $\frac{x}{2} = 15$	**l** $n - 14 = 14$
m $19 - g = 11$	**n** $23 = j + 4$	**o** $15 - f = 7$	**p** $7 = q - 3$

Exercise 20B Two-step equations

1 Use your preferred method to solve these equations.

a $3x + 1 = 13$	**b** $2x + 4 = 18$	**c** $5x + 2 = 27$	**d** $4x + 4 = 12$
e $5x - 2 = 23$	**f** $2x - 8 = 10$	**g** $3x - 2 = 19$	**h** $4x - 9 = 23$
i $7x + 4 = 25$	**j** $6x + 5 = 11$	**k** $9x + 8 = 26$	**l** $8x + 5 = 37$
m $3x - 4 = 8$	**n** $7x - 1 = 34$	**o** $6x - 9 = 9$	**p** $2x - 11 = 13$

2 Solve these equations.

a $3k + 15 = 33$	**b** $9b - 15 = 12$	**c** $5x - 15 = 0$	**d** $8y + 9 = 9$
e $3a - 24 = 0$	**f** $4m + 4 = 40$	**g** $4k + 13 = 17$	**h** $5x - 14 = 41$
i $4x + 3 = 15$	**j** $3a - 12 = 9$	**k** $6m - 1 = 17$	**l** $4w - 9 = 23$
m $11p + 4 = 26$	**n** $10x - 4 = 46$	**o** $7j + 5 = 47$	**p** $3n - 9 = 30$

3 Solve these equations, writing your answers as a fraction or decimal fraction.

a $6x + 5 = 8$	**b** $8x - 1 = 1$	**c** $12x + 5 = 9$	**d** $10x + 13 = 15$
e $8x + 2 = 8$	**f** $9x + 7 = 13$	**g** $15x - 3 = 6$	**h** $24x - 9 = 6$

4 Solve these equations.

a $9 + 4a = 25$ **b** $\frac{x}{3} + 7 = 11$ **c** $12 = 8b - 4$ **d** $\frac{k}{5} + 9 = 12$

e $\frac{y}{2} + 9 = 16$ **f** $8 = 7p - 13$ **g** $18 - 2r = 4$ **h** $\frac{n}{4} + 17 = 19$

i $\frac{z}{3} + 5 = 11$ **j** $25 - 8b = 9$ **k** $15 = 2t - 3$ **l** $7 = 8x + 3$

5 Solve these equations, writing your answer as a fraction or decimal fraction where necessary.

a $7p - 6 = 29$ **b** $3w - 5 = 19$ **c** $52 - 8a + 4$ **d** $31 = 9u + 4$

e $\frac{r}{4} + 19 = 23$ **f** $38 = 5z - 42$ **g** $0 = \frac{g}{3} - 7$ **h** $7e - 49 = 28$

i $6v + 19 = 22$ **j** $\frac{n}{9} + 17 = 18$ **k** $22 = 12j + 18$ **l** $1 = \frac{t}{7} - 4$

m $18q - 9 = 3$ **n** $28 = 40m + 3$ **o** $15b + 7 = 13$ **p** $17 = 48l - 19$

q $6c + 7 = 28$ **r** $14x - 8 = 13$ **s** $34 = \frac{f}{5} + 31$ **t** $30y - 30 = 6$

Exercise 20C Using equations to solve problems

1 I think of a number, multiply it by 3 then add 7. The answer is 19.

   a Write an equation to represent this situation.

   b Solve it to find the number.

2 I think of a number, multiply it by 6 then subtract 17. The result is 37.

   a Write an equation to represent this situation.

   b Solve it to find the number.

3 Robert has 5 more sweets than Daniel. Together they have 23 sweets. Let the number of sweets Daniel has be x.

   a Write an equation to represent this situation in its simplest form.

   b Solve it to find out how many sweets they each have.

4 Mark and Ian collect music. Ian has 24 more vinyl records than Mark. They have a total of 120 records between them. Let x be the number of records owned by Mark.

   a Write an equation to represent this situation in its simplest form.

   b Solve it to find out how many records each person owns.

5 Sarah and Grace earned money selling some old belongings in a car boot sale. Grace earned £16 more than Sarah. They earned £52 in total. Let x be the amount of money Grace earned.

   a Write down and simplify an equation to represent this situation.

   b Solve it to find out the amount of money they each earned.

6 Andrew is twice as old as Chris. Together their ages add up to 81. Let Chris be y years old.

   a Write an equation to represent this situation in its simplest form.

   b Solve it to find out the age of each person.

7 Matthew and Amy went to the beach to collect seashells. Together they collected 35 shells and Amy collected 4 times as many as Matthew.
Let x be the number of shells Matthew collected.

a Write an equation to represent this situation in its simplest form.

b Solve it to find out how many seashells they each collected.

8 Ella and Ross went to pick strawberries on a fruit farm. Ella collected 3 times as many as Ross and together they picked 3600 g.
Let s be the weight of strawberries Ross picked.

a Write an equation to represent this situation in its simplest form.

b Solve it to find out the weight of strawberries picked by each person.

9 In the agricultural show, Banktop Farm won 3 times as many medals for their sheep as Hillside Farm. Together they won 56 medals.
Let m be the number of medals won by Hillside Farm.

a Write an equation to represent this situation in its simplest form.

b Solve it to find out how many medals were won by each farm.

c If Banktop Farm had won 2 more medals then they would have won twice as many as Mossend Farm. How many medals did Mossend Farm win?

10 A train journey from Elgin to Tain takes twice as long as the same journey by car. Together the journeys took 4 hours and 15 minutes.
Let t be the time taken for the car journey in minutes.

a Write an equation to represent this situation in its simplest form.

b Solve it to find out the time taken for each journey in hours and minutes.

11 In last year's football championship, City were 4 points short of earning twice as many points as Rovers. Together they earned 119 points.
Let p be the number of points earned by Rovers.

a Write an equation to represent this situation in its simplest form.

b Solve it to find out the number of points earned by each team.

12 Mac and Jamie went bird spotting. Mac was 2 short of seeing twice as many birds as Jamie. Together they saw 55 birds.
Let b be the number of birds Jamie saw.

a Write an equation to represent this situation in its simplest form.

b Solve it to find out how many birds they each saw.

21 Creating and evaluating formulae

Exercise 21A Evaluating a formula

1 A cashmere company supplies their material from rolls that are 1 m wide. The material costs £45 per metre of length. This is represented by the formula $C = 45l$, where C is the cost in pounds and l is the length in metres. Calculate the cost of buying these lengths of cashmere.

    a 2 m   **b** 5 m   **c** 8 m   **d** 20 m

2 Kathryn has a small business buying and selling antique furniture. To make money, she adds a fixed profit of £50 to each item she sells. The selling price for each item is calculated using the formula $S = P + 50$, where S is the selling price and P is the price she paid for each item. Calculate her selling price for items that cost:

    a £50   **b** £85   **c** £320   **d** £1245

3 The cost of hiring a community hall and providing food for a party is given by the formula $C = 200 + 15g$, where C is the cost in pounds and g is the number of guests. How much would it cost to have a party with the following numbers of guests?

    a 10   **b** 25   **c** 40   **d** 120

4 A plumber charges £22 per hour plus a call-out charge of £40. The formula to calculate the cost of a job is $C = 22h + 40$, where h is the amount of time, in hours, she takes to complete the job. Calculate how much she would charge for a job that takes:

    a 1 hour   **b** 3 hours

    c 5 hours   **d** 3 days (assume she works for 8 hours per day).

5 The cooking time for a joint of beef is 25 minutes per 450 g plus an extra 25 minutes. This can be represented using the formula $t = \dfrac{W + 450}{18}$, where t is the time in minutes and W is the weight in grams. Calculate the cooking time for a joint that weighs:

    a 450 g   **b** 900 g   **c** 4050 g   **d** 2.25 kg

6 The cost of hiring a car is £30 per day plus 30 p per mile. This can be represented by the formula $C = 30d + 0.3m$, where d is the number of days and m is the distance travelled in miles. Find C, the cost of hiring a car, for:

    a 2 days travelling 100 miles   **b** 5 days travelling 180 miles

    c 1 week travelling 650 miles   **d** 2 weeks travelling 1000 miles

Exercise 21B Finding other variables

1 Simon was organising a visit to a forest theme park for a group of people and made sandwiches for their lunch. The number of sandwiches he made was given by the formula $S = 2p + 8$, where S is the number of sandwiches and p is the number of people. How many people were in his group if he made these numbers of sandwiches?

    a 32   **b** 50   **c** 78

2 The Johnston family are buying a new carpet for their living room. Carpet King charge £18 per square metre plus £35 for fitting. This is represented by the formula $C = 18a + 35$, where C is the total cost and a is the area of the room. Calculate the area of the room if the carpet cost:

a £251   **b** £485   **c** £791

3 The cost of hiring a community hall and providing food for a party is given by the formula $C = 200 + 15g$, where C is the total cost and g is the number of guests. Find how many guests you could invite if your budget is:

a £350   **b** £500   **c** £950   **d** £750

4 Amanda paints pottery items in a factory and is paid by the amount she produces. Her pay is represented by the formula $P = 25i + 375$, where P is her pay in pence and i is the number of pottery items. Calculate how many items she needs to produce to be paid:

a £10   **b** £50   **c** £70

5 The cost of a taxi fare is £1.10 plus 22 p per tenth of a mile. This can be represented by the formula $C = 1.1 + 2.2n$, where C is the total cost and n is the number of miles.

a Calculate the cost of a journey of 15 miles.

b How far can you travel by taxi for £10?

Exercise 21C Creating a formula from a table of values

1 Granny makes tea when she has visitors. The amount of tea she puts in the pot is given below.

Number of visitors, V	1	2	3	4	5
Number of spoons of tea, T	4	6	8	10	12

Find a formula for the number of spoons of tea, T, when you know the number of visitors, V.

> **Hint** Use the same method you used for the sequences in Exercise 18B.

2 The amount charged by a gardener depends on the amount of time he spends on the job.

Time (hours), t	1	2	3	4	5
Charge (£), C	35	50	65	80	95

Find a formula for the charge, C, when you know the time taken for the job, t.

3 A pattern is made up from circles and trapeziums, as shown in the diagram.

 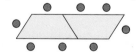 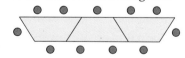

The table shows the number of trapeziums and circles in each pattern.

Number of trapeziums, T	1	2	3	4	5
Number of circles, C	5	8	11	14	17

Find a formula for the number of circles, C, when you know the number of trapeziums, T.

4 A paving pattern is made up from rectangular black slabs and smaller square slabs, as shown.

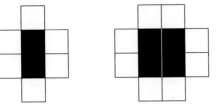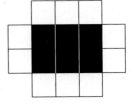

a Copy and complete the table.

Number of black slabs, B	1	2	3	4	5		10
Number of white slabs, W	6	8	10				

b Find a formula for the number of white slabs, W, when you know the number of black slabs, B.

c If a stretch of paving has 85 black slabs, how many white slabs does it have?

d If a stretch of paving has 112 white slabs, how many black slabs does it have?

5 Write a formula for y when you know x for each of the following.

a

x	1	2	3	4	5
y	3	5	7	9	11

b

x	1	2	3	4	5
y	2	5	8	11	14

c

x	0	1	2	3	4
y	3	7	11	15	19

d

x	0	1	2	3	4
y	−2	3	8	13	18

Exercise 21D Creating a formula to represent a statement or problem

1 Ailsa is 7 years older than her sister Flora. Construct a formula to find Alisa's age, A, if you know Flora's age, F.

2 John's guitar teacher charges £25 per hour for guitar lessons.

a Construct a formula for the cost, C, if you know the number of hours of lessons, h.

b Calculate the cost of 8 hours of lessons.

3 A travel agent will give you an exchange rate of 1.32 dollars for each pound you give them.

a Construct a formula for the number of dollars, D, you get for P pounds.

b How many dollars do you get if you exchange £50?

4 Al uses 3 cups of water per cup of porridge oats plus 1 extra cup of water to make his perfect porridge.

a Construct a formula for the number of cups of water, W, needed for x cups of porridge oats.

b How many cups of water are needed for 4 cups of oats?

5 A printing company charges 25 p per card plus a setup charge of £8 to print party invitations.

a Construct a formula for the total cost, C, in pounds (£), of printing g cards.

b Calculate the cost of printing 75 cards.

22 Drawing 2D shapes

Exercise 22A Constructing triangles

1 Accurately construct each of the following triangles and then measure and label the side marked with a letter.

a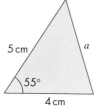

b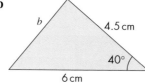

c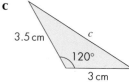

d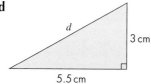

e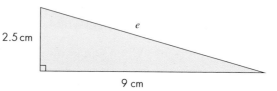

2 Accurately construct each of the following triangles and then measure and label the side marked with a letter.

a

b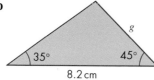

c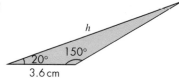

3 Accurately construct each of the following triangles and then measure and label the angle marked with a letter.

a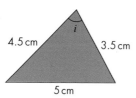

b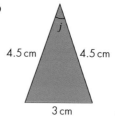

c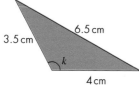

d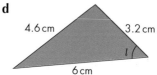

4 Accurately construct each of the following triangles and measure the labelled side or angle.

a

70°
4 cm
m
50°

b
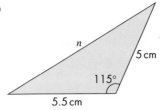
n
5 cm
115°
5.5 cm

c

4 cm
4.7 cm
o
2.5 cm

d
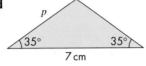
p
35°
35°
7 cm

Exercise 22B Constructing other 2D shapes

1 **a** Construct the parallelogram *ABCD*.

   b Measure and label the lengths of sides *BC* and *CD* to the nearest millimetre.

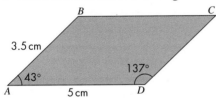
B   *C*
3.5 cm
137°
43°
A   5 cm   *D*

2 Construct the trapezium *EFGH*.

   a Measure and label the lengths of sides *EF* and *FG* to the nearest millimetre.

   b Measure and label the size of angle *EFG* to the nearest degree.

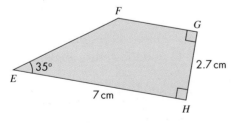
F
G
35°
2.7 cm
E
7 cm
H

3 **a** Construct the quadrilateral *JKLM*.

   b Measure and label the length of side *KL* and the size of ∠*JKL*.

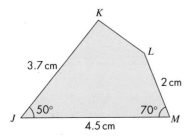
K
L
3.7 cm
2 cm
50°   70°
J   *M*
4.5 cm

> **Hint** ∠*JKL* is the angle formed where the lines *JK* and *KL* meet.

4 **a** Construct the quadrilateral *NOPQ*.

    b Measure and label the size of ∠*NOP*, ∠*NQP* and ∠*OPQ*.

    c Name the quadrilateral *NOPQ*.

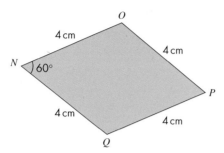

5 **a** Construct the quadrilateral *RSTU*.

    b Measure and label the size of ∠*RST* and ∠*STU*.

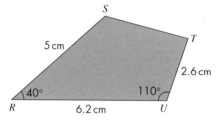

6 **a** Construct the polygon *ABCDE*.

    b Measure and label the length of side *BC* and the size of ∠*ABC*.

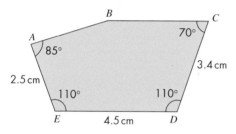

7 **a** Draw a circle with a radius of 5 cm and use it to construct a regular polygon with 9 sides.

> **Hint** Divide 360° by the number of sides to find the centre angle.

    b Measure and label the side length of your polygon to the nearest millimetre.

23 Angles and angle rules

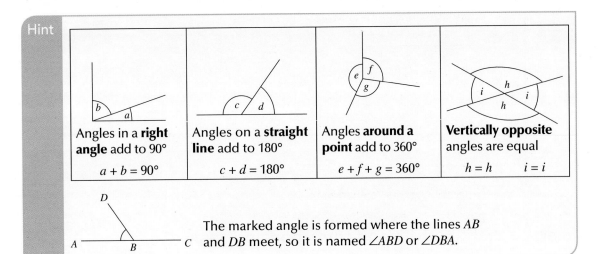

Angles in a **right angle** add to 90°
$$a + b = 90°$$

Angles on a **straight line** add to 180°
$$c + d = 180°$$

Angles **around a point** add to 360°
$$e + f + g = 360°$$

Vertically opposite angles are equal
$$h = h \qquad i = i$$

The marked angle is formed where the lines *AB* and *DB* meet, so it is named ∠*ABD* or ∠*DBA*.

Exercise 23A Calculating angles

1 Name these unknown angles and calculate their value.

a

b

c

d

2 Calculate the size of these unknown angles.

a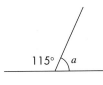

b

c

d

3 Calculate the size of these unknown angles.

a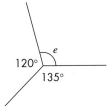

b

c

d

4 Name all the unknown angles marked with an angle arc and calculate their value.

a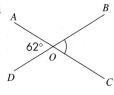

b

c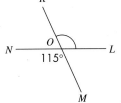

d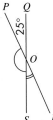

5   Calculate the size of these unknown angles.

a
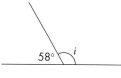

b

c
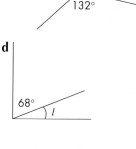

d

Exercise 23B Alternate and corresponding angles

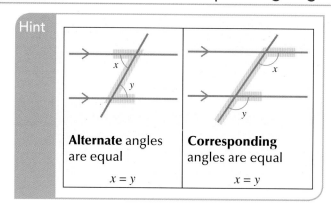

Hint

Alternate angles are equal

$x = y$

Corresponding angles are equal

$x = y$

1   Calculate the size of the unknown angles.

a

b
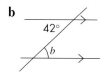

c
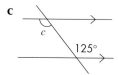

d
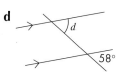

e
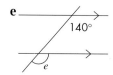

f
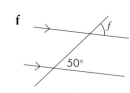

g
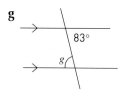

h
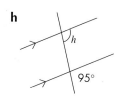

i
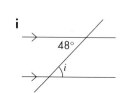

2 Calculate the sizes of these unknown angles.

a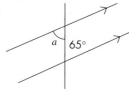

b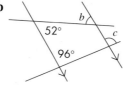

c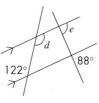

d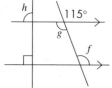

e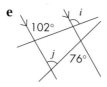

f

g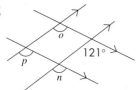

h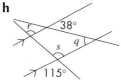

i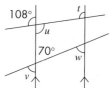

Exercise 23C Angles in a triangle

1 Calculate the size of the unknown angles in each of these triangles.

a

b

c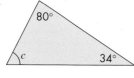

d

e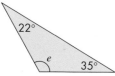

f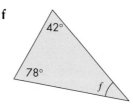

Hint Remember: angles in a triangle add to 180°.

2 Calculate the size of the unknown angles in these triangles.

a

b

c

d

e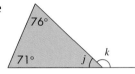

f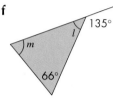

g

h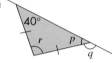

i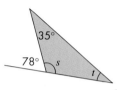

Hint | Angles opposite sides of equal length in an isosceles triangle are equal.

Exercise 23D Angles in quadrilaterals and polygons

1
i Calculate the size of the unknown angles in these quadrilaterals.

ii Identify which diagrams show a trapezium, a parallelogram and a kite.

a

b

c

d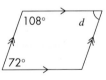

e

f

g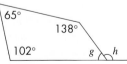

h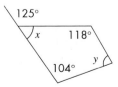

Hint | Remember that angles in a quadrilateral add to 360°.

Example 23.1

Calculate the size of the unknown angle in this polygon.

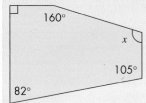

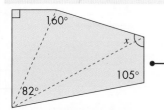

The shape has 5 sides, so it can be split up into three triangles by drawing lines from one of its vertices. The sum of its interior angles is 3 × 180°.

Sum of interior angles = 3 × 180° = 540°

90° + 160° + 105° + 82° = 437° ●——— Add the interior angles you know to find their total.

$x + 437° = 540°$

$x = 540° - 437° = 103°$

2 Calculate the size of the unknown angles in these polygons.

a

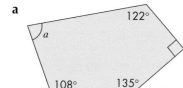

b

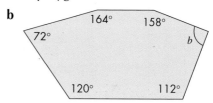

24 Scale and bearings

Exercise 24A Scale drawings and map scales

1 The diagram shows a scale drawing of a classroom, using a scale of 1 cm to 2 m.

  a Find the actual length of the classroom.

  b Find the actual breadth of the classroom.

2 The diagram is a scale drawing of a village community hall. The hall is 25 m long.

  a Find the scale used in the drawing.

  b Find the breadth of the hall.

  c Calculate the perimeter of the hall.

3 The diagram shows the floor plan of Dan's shed, using a scale of 2 cm to 1 m.

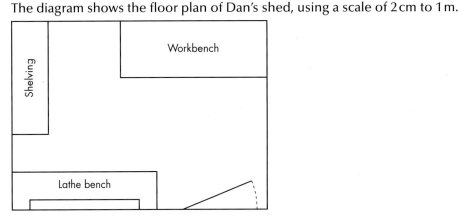

  a Calculate the length and breadth of the shed.

  b Find the length of the workbench.

  c Dan wants to lay flooring on the parts of the floor not covered by benches or shelving.

  Calculate the area of flooring he will need to buy.

4 Write each of these map scales as a ratio.

  a 1 cm to 300 m   **b** 1 cm to 10 m   **c** 2 cm to 1 m

  d 4 cm to 1 km   **e** 2 cm to 30 m

  > **Hint** Your answers should have a format such as 1 : 25 000, 1 : 50 000, and so on.

5 The map shows part of south-east England.

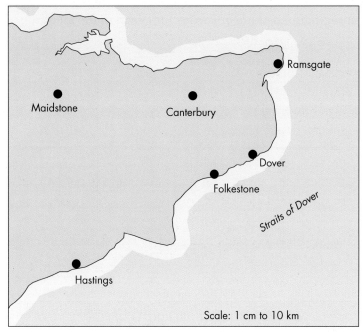

Scale: 1 cm to 10 km

a Using the map scale of 1 cm to 10 km, find the actual direct distances between:

  i Maidstone and Folkestone

  ii Canterbury and Dover

  iii Hastings and Ramsgate

b Sarah lives in Canterbury. She drove to Dover to pick up some friends from the ferry then went to Hastings for the day before returning home. Calculate the total direct distance between the places she travelled. The trip meter in her car showed more than this. Why?

6 The map shows Edinburgh city centre. The scale used is 1 cm : 100 m.

Find the real-life shortest distances between:

a Princes Mall and Adam House

b Edinburgh Rail station and City Art Centre

c Edinburgh Dungeon and the Sheriff Court.

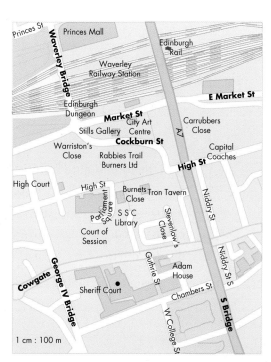

1 cm : 100 m

Exercise 24B Bearings

1 Write down the three-figure bearing of *B* from *A* for each of the following.

a

b

c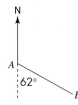

d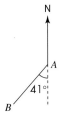

e

f

Hint	Bearings are measured clockwise from north and are always given using three digits. If the angle is less than 100° then add a leading 0, so an angle of 64° would be a bearing of 064°.

2 The following diagrams show the positions of two locations on a map.

a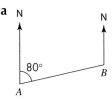

b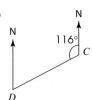

c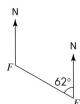

d

Find the three-figure bearing of each of the following.

a i *B* from *A*   **ii** *A* from *B*

b i *D* from *C*   **ii** *C* from *D*

c i *F* from *E*   **ii** *E* from *F*

d i *H* from *G*   **ii** *G* from *H*.

3 A ship sails from harbour H to port P. It then sails to port Q before returning to the harbour, as shown in the scale diagram below. The scale used is 1 cm to 50 km.

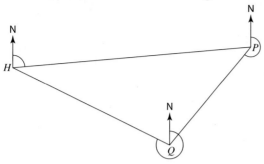

Find the following:

a the bearing of P from H **b** the bearing of Q from P

c the bearing of H from Q **d** the total distance travelled on the journey.

4 The map shows the area around Inverness on a scale of 1 cm : 1 km.

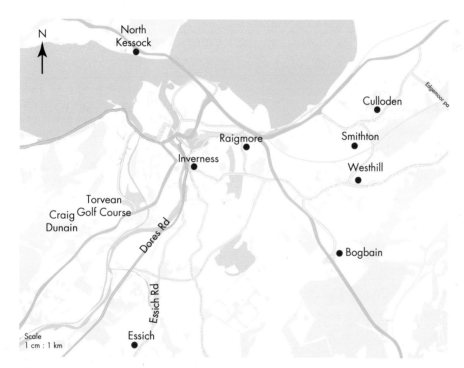

Use the map to answer these questions.

a What place is 4.6 km away from Inverness on a bearing of 121°?

b What distance and bearing is Culloden from Bogbain?

c If you travelled 3.4 km from Inverness on a bearing of 335°, where would you end up?

5 A helicopter leaves Osprey and travels on a bearing of 080° for 60 km to reach Arton. It then heads due south for 48 km to Blair, before finally returning directly to Osprey.

a Make an accurate scale drawing of the helicopter's journey. Use a scale of 1 cm to 12 km and clearly mark the bearings and distances in centimetres on your drawing.

b What distance and bearing does the helicopter travel from Blair to Osprey?

25 Enlargement and reduction

Exercise 25A Scale factor

Example 25.1

Shape **A** is enlarged to shape **B**. Calculate the scale factor of the enlargement.

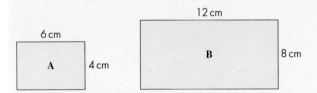

Length of top side of **A** (original length): 6 cm

Length of top side of **B** (enlarged length): 12 cm

> Always use a pair of corresponding sides to find the scale factor. You could use the 4 cm and 8 cm sides to get the same answer.

$$\text{Scale factor} = \frac{\text{enlarged length}}{\text{original length}} = \frac{12}{6} = 2$$

1 Calculate the scale factor of the enlargements for the following pairs of shapes.

a

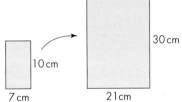

b

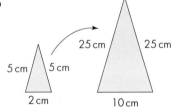

c

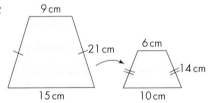

d

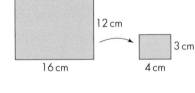

e

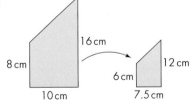

f

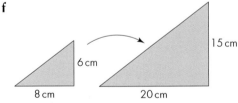

2 A TV with an advertised screen size of 40 inches has a length of 88.6 cm and a height of 49.8 cm. A 60-inch model of the same TV measures 132.9 cm by 74.7 cm. Find the scale factor of the enlargement from the 40-inch TV to the 60-inch TV.

3 A guitar maker offers a full-sized model that is 98 cm long and 33 cm across the widest part of its body. They also make a student model that is 73.5 cm long and 24.75 cm wide. What is the scale factor used to make the smaller guitar from the larger original?

4 A poster on a bus stop advertising a new best-selling novel measures 132 cm by 88 cm. The actual novel is 24 cm tall and 16 cm wide. What scale factor was used to enlarge the book to the advert?

5 A photo booth can print your pictures in several different sizes:

   4 cm × 6 cm   8 cm × 10 cm   5 cm × 7 cm   8 cm × 12 cm   6 cm × 8 cm

If 4 cm × 6 cm is the original size, which other size is a true enlargement?

Exercise 25B Enlargements and reductions

1 Draw an enlargement of these shapes by a scale factor of 2.

a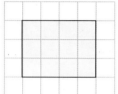

b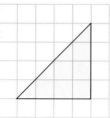

c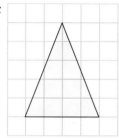

d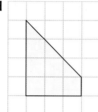

2 Draw a reduction of these shapes by a scale factor of $\frac{1}{2}$

a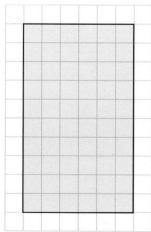

b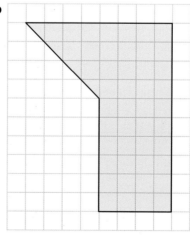

> **Hint** A scale factor less than 1 means the new shape is smaller than the original shape.

3 Draw each shape. Then:

   i reduce it by a scale factor of $\frac{1}{3}$ **ii** enlarge it by a scale factor of 2.

a
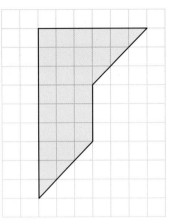

b
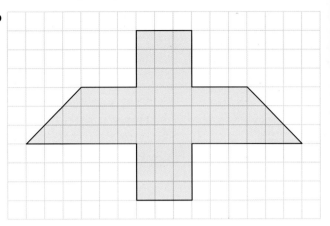

4 Draw this shape. Then:

   a enlarge it by a scale factor of 3

   b reduce it by a scale factor of $\frac{1}{4}$

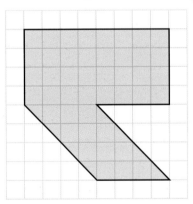

5 Draw this shape. Then:

   a reduce it by a scale factor of $\frac{3}{4}$

   b enlarge it by a scale factor of $1\frac{1}{2}$

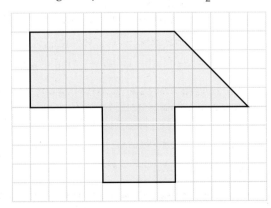

26 Coordinates

Exercise 26A Plotting coordinates

1 Write down the coordinates of the points labelled A to G on the following diagram.

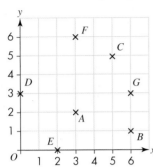

> **Hint** Coordinates are always written with the x value before the y value, separated by a comma, and with brackets around them: (x, y).

2 Plot the following sets of points on separate coordinate grids, with x- and y- axes from 0 to 6. Join the plotted points to make a 2D shape. Write down the mathematical name of each shape.

a (1, 1), (5, 6) and (5, 1)

b (1, 3), (6, 3), (4, 1) and (3, 1)

c (0, 3), (3, 6), (5, 4) and (2, 1)

d (2, 1), (2, 5), (5, 4) and (5, 0)

e (1, 2), (3, 5), (6, 3) and (4, 0)

f (1, 1), (1, 5) and (6, 3)

3 Look at the grid shown.

a Write down the coordinates of A, B and C.

b The points A, B and C form three vertices of a square. Write down the coordinates of the fourth vertex, D.

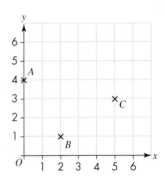

4 Look at the grid shown.

a Write down the coordinates of A, B and C.

b The points A, B and C form three vertices of a rhombus. Write down the coordinates of the fourth vertex, D.

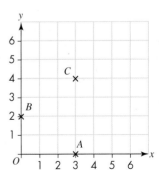

5 Make a copy of the grid shown.

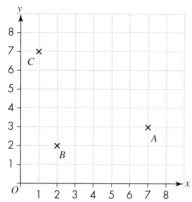

a Write down the coordinates of A, B and C.

b The points A, B and C form three vertices of a square. Plot the fourth vertex,
D, and write down its coordinates.

c Draw in the diagonals of the square.
Write down the coordinates of the point where the diagonals intersect.

6 The points A(2, 4), B(2, 8) and C(6, 8) form three vertices of the quadrilateral ABCD.
Find:

a the coordinates of D if ABCD is a square

b all possible coordinates of D if ABCD is a kite.

7 The points (2, 2) and (6, 4) are two vertices of the square ABCD.

Find the coordinates of the other two vertices if these points are:

a A and B   b A and C

Exercise 26B Using coordinates

**For Questions 1 to 3, draw coordinate axes for x and y from 0 to 8 on centimetre squared paper then plot
the coordinates. Join them to form a 2D shape and find the area of the shape.**

1 a ABC with A(1, 2), B(7, 2) and C(4, 7)

b DEF with D(3, 1), E(3, 5) and F(6, 5)

c GHI with G(1, 3), H(4, 8) and I(5, 3)

> Hint   Use the formulae from Chapter 15 to find the area of each shape.

2 a Parallelogram ABCD with A(2, 1), B(4, 4), C(8, 4) and D(6, 1)

b Parallelogram EFGH with E(0, 3), F(3, 8), G(8, 8) and H(5, 3)

c Parallelogram IJKL with I(1, 1), J(1, 5), K(5, 7) and L(5, 3)

3 a Trapezium ABCD with A(2, 2), B(4, 6), C(7, 6) and D(8, 2)

b Trapezium EFGH with E(1, 6), F(7, 6), G(5, 2) and H(3, 2)

c Trapezium IJKL with I(1, 2), J(1, 7), K(6, 6) and L(6, 2)

4 Copy the triangle *ABC* onto squared paper. Label it **P**.

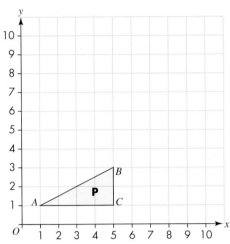

a Translate triangle **P** 2 units right and 5 units up. Label the new triangle **Q** and write down the coordinates of its vertices.

b Translate triangle **Q** 3 units right and 2 units down. Label the new triangle **R** and write down the coordinates of its vertices.

c Describe the translation that takes triangle **R** back onto triangle **P**.

> **Hint** When a shape is translated, every point on the shape moves the same distance.

5 Copy the following diagrams onto centimetre squared paper with *x*- and *y*-axes from 0 to 12. Enlarge each shape by the given scale factor, using *O* as the centre of enlargement.

a Scale factor 3   **b** Scale factor 2   **c** Scale factor 3

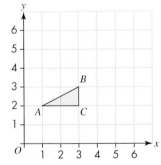 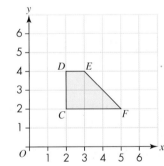 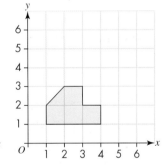

> **Hint** For a scale factor of 2, all the points on the image will be twice the distance from the origin, *O*.

27 Symmetry and reflection

Exercise 27A Symmetry and reflection

1 Copy each shape. Draw its lines of symmetry, where they exist.

a
b
c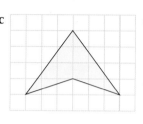
d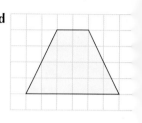

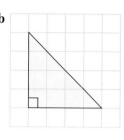

e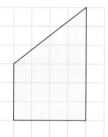
f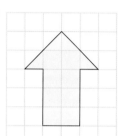
g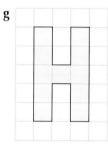
h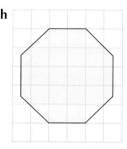

2 Copy each diagram onto squared paper. Draw in its reflection in the given mirror line.

a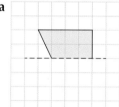
b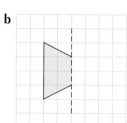
c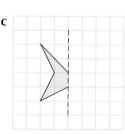
d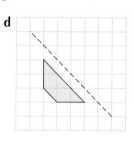

3 Copy these shapes onto squared paper and draw in their reflection in the given mirror line.

a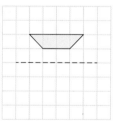
b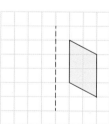
c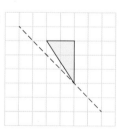
d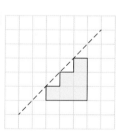

e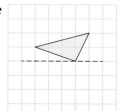
f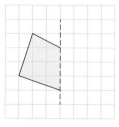
g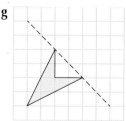
h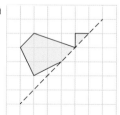

4 Copy these shapes onto squared paper and draw in their reflection in the given mirror line.

a

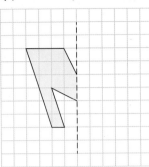

b

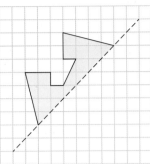

Exercise 27B Reflection in two mirror lines

1 Copy each of the following shapes onto squared paper. Reflect it in one of the mirror lines. Then reflect both shapes in the second mirror line.

a

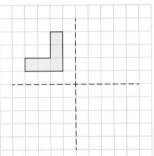

b

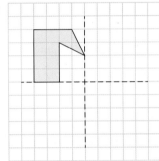

2 Copy each of the following shapes onto squared paper. Reflect it in one of the mirror lines. Then reflect both shapes in the second mirror line.

a

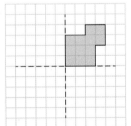

b

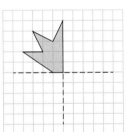

c

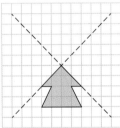

d

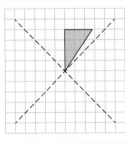

e

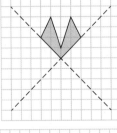

f

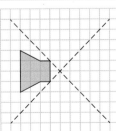

g

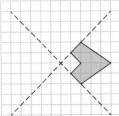

h

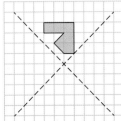

i

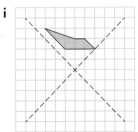

28 Interpreting data

Exercise 28A Interpreting charts and tables

 1 The following chart shows the distances, in miles, between some towns and cities in Scotland.

Wick

103	**Inverness**					
204	105	**Aberdeen**				
213	112	88	**Perth**			
244	143	121	37	**Stirling**		
256	155	127	44	38	**Edinburgh**	
269	168	146	63	27	46	**Glasgow**

a How far is it from Wick to Stirling?

b How far is it from Edinburgh to Aberdeen?

c Which two places are 168 miles apart?

d Which place is 213 miles from Perth?

 2 The table shows the films in the Playhouse Cinema for this week.

Film title	Fri	Sat	Sun	Mon	Tue	Wed	Thu
Vans 3	✓	✓			✓	✓	✓
Terrible Me Too		✓	✓				
The Amazing Bird Man	✓	✓	✓	✓		✓	✓
Galaxy Trek	✓			✓	✓	✓	✓

a On which days can you watch *Vans 3*?

b Which film is on most often?

c Which film only shows at the weekend?

d Which films could you see on a Wednesday?

 3 The table shows the sales of different ice cream flavours in two weeks in the summer.

Ice cream flavours	Week 1 sales (litres)	Week 2 sales (litres)
Strawberry swirl	15	24
Chocolate fudge	12	11
Pure vanilla	23	24
Mint madness	9	18
Honeycomb heaven	13	13

a How much chocolate fudge flavour was sold in week 1?

b Which flavours sold more in week 2 than in week 1?

c Which was the most popular flavour overall?

d In which week was more ice cream sold? How much more?

4 A championship medal table is shown below.

Country	Gold	Silver	Bronze
USA	9	6	2
Jamaica	2	7	3
China	6	7	4
United Kingdom	3	3	2
France	2	4	3

a Which country won the most gold medals?

b How many medals did Jamaica win?

c Which countries won the same number of medals overall?

d If a gold medal scores 3 points, a silver 2 points and a bronze 1 point, how many points did the United Kingdom score?

5 The table shows the arm span measurements for a group of S2 pupils.

Arm span (cm)	Girls	Boys
140–149	3	4
150–159	5	1
160–169	4	6
170–179	2	4
180–189	1	0

a How many boys had arm spans between 160 and 169 cm?

b What was the most common arm span group for girls?

c Did a girl or boy have the longest arms?

d Overall, did girls or boys have longer arm spans?

Exercise 28B Interpreting graphs and diagrams

1 Simon carried out a survey to find out the colour of cars passing his house in 1 hour on both Saturday and Sunday. His results are shown in the bar chart.

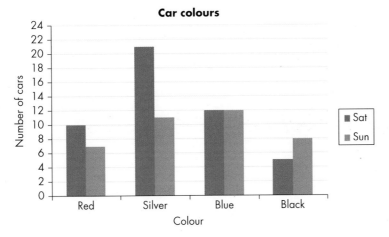

a How many blue cars passed his house?

b What was the most common colour?

c How many cars passed on Saturday?

d How many more silver cars were there than red cars?

e Is there any difference in traffic between Saturday and Sunday?

2 The results of a survey to find out the most popular pets are shown in the pie chart below.

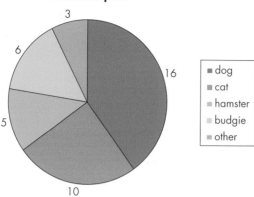

Favourite pets

- dog
- cat
- hamster
- budgie
- other

a How many people owned a cat?

b How many pet owners were there altogether?

c Alan said that 'most pet owners own a dog'. Is he correct?

3 A survey was carried out to find out the main reason people shop at a supermarket. The results are shown in the following chart.

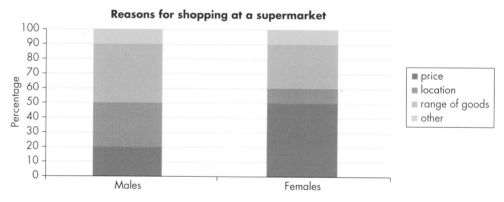

Reasons for shopping at a supermarket

- price
- location
- range of goods
- other

a Which gender thought price was the main reason?

b What was the main reason for the other gender?

c What percentage of males said the range of goods was the main reason?

d Location was given as the main reason by a higher percentage of males than females. What was the difference in percentage?

4 The reaction times in milliseconds (ms) of a group of S2 pupils are shown in the following chart.

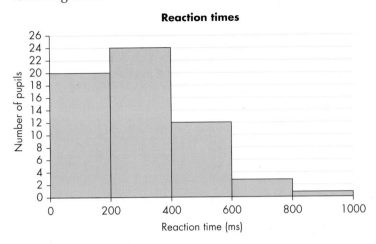

Reaction times

a Which group contains the largest number of data items?

b How many pupils had a reaction time between 0 and 200 ms?

c How many pupils had a reaction time of less than 600 ms?

d How many pupils were in the group sampled?

5 An advertisement for an electrical retailer used the headline 'Dramatic rise in 4K TV sales' and included the following graph to support their claim.

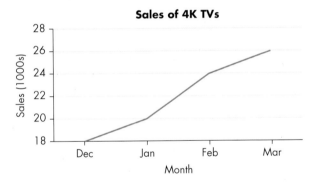

Sales of 4K TVs

a Give a reason why this graph is misleading and explain the effect this has.

b Draw a graph to correctly illustrate this data. Is the headline still valid?

6 A pet food company claims that 'Mutt Crunch is more popular with dogs than any other brand', as shown in this graph.

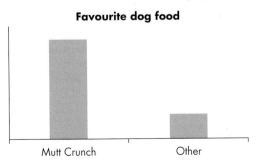

Favourite dog food

Is this a reasonable claim to make? How could the graph be improved?

29 Collecting data

Exercise 29A Sampling and bias

1 A head teacher wants to sample the opinions of some students about after-school clubs. There are 310 boys and 190 girls in the school and he wants a sample of 50 students. The deputy suggests selecting 25 boys and 25 girls at random from an alphabetical list of students.

a Explain why the sample should not contain 25 boys and 25 girls.

b Suggest a better way to select the sample.

> **Hint** A **sample** should reflect the whole population it represents.

2 Comment on the sample size mentioned in these advertising campaigns.

a An advert for sun cream claimed it absorbed up to 90% of harmful UV rays. The small print on the advert stated that '84% of 43 consumers agreed'.

b The slogan on an advert for cat food claimed that 'In our tests, 8 out of 10 cat owners who expressed a preference said their cats preferred it'.

3 Read the following situations. Suggest why they could produce biased data and how you could improve them to get unbiased responses.

a Asking people leaving a burger restaurant what type of fast food they prefer.

b Asking members of a gardening club if they preferred home-grown vegetables.

c Asking the boys football team if they thought girls or boys were better at football.

d Asking school pupils if they should be given more pocket money.

e Asking the question 'Do you agree that criminals should be locked up for longer?'

f Asking a class of pupils how many cigarettes they smoke in a week.

> **Hint** **Biased** data does not represent the whole population; an unbiased response is not influenced by the question that is asked or the sample that is surveyed.

Exercise 29B Data collection methods

1 Stephanie wants to find out about TV viewing habits of pupils at her school. She has designed four questions:

i What gender are you? (please tick)   M ☐   F ☐

ii How old are you?

iii How much TV do you watch?

iv What do you think about current TV?

Is each of these questions statistically well written? Give a reason for your answer and suggest a way of improving those that are not.

2 Here are some different data collection methods:

- construct a questionnaire
- do research on the internet
- carry out an experiment
- use a software database (e.g. an encyclopaedia CD)
- visit a library for books or other print sources.

Which methods would you use to investigate these questions?

a Which Year group is better at arriving at school on time?

b Did the GB squad win more medals in the last Olympics than they have at any other Olympics?

c Does the time of year have any effect on the number of people using the school canteen at lunchtime?

d Which band is the most popular among school pupils?

e Are teenagers taller now than 30 years ago?

f Do the best-selling modern novels have a shorter word length than older classic novels such as Walter Scott, Robert Louis Stevenson, Charles Dickens, Emily Brontë, etc.?

3 Peter wants to find out if the traffic on the road outside his house is busier at the weekend or during the week. He decides to record the number of cars passing his house for 1 hour on a Thursday evening and repeats the experiment again on the following Sunday morning. After analysing the results, he concludes that traffic is busier during the week.

a Does his conclusion give a true reflection of the amount of traffic on Peter's road? Give reasons for your answer.

b What could he do to improve his results?

30 Displaying data

Exercise 30A Creating graphs, charts and diagrams

1 Construct bar charts from these frequency tables.

a The colour of cars in a traffic survey

Colour	Frequency
Red	15
Blue	22
Black	8
Silver	11
Green	4

b The most popular type of TV programme

Type of programme	Frequency
Drama	15
Entertainment	26
Sport	18
Film	12
News	8
Reality	6

Hint Remember to check you have done the following when you construct a chart or graph:

- included a title
- labelled axes clearly
- have correctly labelled scales on axes
- drawn axes/lines with a ruler.

2 Construct a line graph for each of these sets of data.

a The average monthly temperature in Glasgow

Month	Jan	Feb	Mar	Apr	May	Jun	Jul	Aug	Sep	Oct	Nov	Dec
Temperature (°C)	3	4	5.5	8	10.5	13.5	15	15	12.5	9.5	6	4.5

b Sales of vinyl records in the UK

Year	2010	2011	2012	2013	2014
Sales (1000s)	230	340	390	780	1290

3 Construct a pie chart to represent each of these sets of data.

a Favourite lunch choices at school

Lunch choice	Roast beef	Chicken pie	Fish fingers	Haggis	Pasta bake
Frequency	6	8	21	14	11

b Top selling ice cream flavour

Ice cream flavour	Strawberry swirl	Chocolate fudge	Pure vanilla	Mint madness	Honeycomb heaven
Frequency	15	12	23	9	13

4 The table shows the arm spans of a group of S2 pupils.

Arm span (cm)	Frequency
140 ⩽ arm span < 150	3
150 ⩽ arm span < 160	8
160 ⩽ arm span < 170	11
170 ⩽ arm span < 180	6
180 ⩽ arm span < 190	2

a Draw a histogram to show the data in the table.

b How many pupils' arm spans are longer than 170 cm?

c What can you say about the arm span of the pupil with the longest arm span?

5 The table shows the heights of some Christmas trees for sale at a farm.

Tree height (m)	Frequency
1.0 ⩽ height < 1.2	8
1.2 ⩽ height < 1.4	7
1.4 ⩽ height < 1.6	24
1.6 ⩽ height < 1.8	18
1.8 ⩽ height < 2.0	15

a Draw a histogram to show the data in the table.

b Which group gives you the most choice of trees?

c Susan needed a tree shorter than 140 cm to fit in her room. How many trees did she have to choose from?

6 a Copy and complete the table to convert weights between metric kilograms and imperial pounds.

Kilograms (kg)	1	2	5	10	25
Pounds (lb)	2.2	4.4			

b Use the data in the table to draw a conversion graph from kilograms to pounds.

c Use your graph to convert these weights into pounds.

  i 15 kg   ii 20 kg   iii 30 kg

d Use your graph to convert these weights into kilograms. Give your answer to the nearest kilogram.

  i 15 lb   ii 35 lb   iii 50 lb

Exercise 30B Choosing data displays

1 Some households were asked how often they recycled their household waste. The results are shown in the table.

a Draw a suitable diagram to represent this data.

b How many households recycled either most weeks or every week?

How often?	Frequency
Every week	25
Most weeks	39
Some weeks	14
Not very often	8
Never	4

2 The table shows the remaining wild populations of some of the most endangered animals in the world.

Animal	Population
Amur leopard	40
Javan rhinoceros	60
Panther	80
Red wolf	100
Californian condor	130

Draw a suitable diagram to illustrate this data.

3 The table shows the sales, in thousands of pounds, for two sportswear companies over a 5-year period.

Year	2013	2014	2015	2016	2017
Sportz 4 All (£ 000s)	10	8	7	5	11
BG Sports (£ 000s)	3	6	7	8	9

a Draw a suitable diagram to illustrate this data.

b In which year(s) did the two companies have the same amount of sales?

c Which company ended this period with the higher sales figure?

d Describe the trend in sales for the two companies over this time period.

4 The table shows the number of branches run by five different banks for two different years.

Bank	2011	2016
Ecosse Bank	2100	1400
Borders Bank	1600	1300
Bank of Forres	1200	1000
Highlands & Islands Bank	1400	800
Central Belt Bank	2900	2000

a Draw a suitable diagram to show the number of branches each bank had in 2011.

b Repeat this for the number of branches in 2016.

c Compare and comment on the number of branches run in 2011 and 2016.

d Which bank closed the fewest number of branches?

5 Lucas recorded the number of minutes his bus arrived late over a 3-week period.

7	12	5	3	11	0	19	2	8	4	0
1	6	2	0	7	14	6	13	16	3	

a Sort the data into a grouped frequency table with a class width of 5.

b Draw a suitable diagram to illustrate his data.

c How many times was his bus more than 10 minutes late?

6 The tables below show the results for two events in an inter-school athletics competition.

i The boys' 100 m

Time (s)	Frequency
$11.5 \leqslant \text{time} < 12.0$	2
$12.0 \leqslant \text{time} < 12.5$	6
$12.5 \leqslant \text{time} < 13.0$	9
$13.0 \leqslant \text{time} < 13.5$	8
$13.5 \leqslant \text{time} < 14.0$	7

ii The girls' hammer

Distance (m)	Frequency
$15 \leqslant \text{distance} < 20$	5
$20 \leqslant \text{distance} < 25$	16
$25 \leqslant \text{distance} < 30$	8
$30 \leqslant \text{distance} < 35$	2
$35 \leqslant \text{distance} < 40$	1

a Draw suitable diagrams to illustrate the results in each event.

b How many:

  i boys were faster than 12.5 seconds?   **ii** girls threw more than 30 m?

7 The following table shows data on CO_2 emissions and life expectancy in the different regions around the world.

Region	CO_2 emissions (tonnes per person)	Life expectancy (years)
A	4.9	66
B	4.1	63
C	7.4	71
D	9.0	61
E	0.4	54
F	0.7	49

a Draw suitable diagrams to illustrate:

  i the amount of CO_2 produced by each region

  ii the life expectancy in each region.

b Comment on each of your graphs, stating clearly which regions have the highest and lowest CO_2 emissions and life expectancy. Does anything surprise you?

31 Probability

Exercise 31A Calculating probabilities

1 Copy the probability scale shown below.

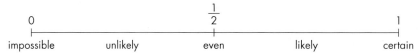

Place these events in the correct position on the probability scale and write their probabilities on the scale as fractions, where possible.

A A person chosen at random was born on a weekday.

B You will wake up tomorrow.

C The score when you roll a dice is less than 5.

D The next baby born will be a boy.

E You will visit space in your lifetime.

F A card picked from a full pack of cards is a heart.

2 A bag contains 12 counters. 5 are blue, 4 are green and 3 are yellow. A counter is picked at random from the bag. Calculate the probability that the counter is:

a green   **b** blue

c blue or yellow   **d** red

e not yellow

> **Hint** Probability of an event happening
>
> $= \dfrac{\text{number of successful outcomes}}{\text{total number of possible outcomes}}$

3 A collection of coins is put in a bag. There are eight 50p coins, five 10p coins, ten 2p coins, five 20p coins and eight 1p coins in the bag. Find the probability that a coin picked at random:

a is a silver coin   **b** is not a 2p

c is a 1p or a 2p   **d** has a value less than 20p.

4 A lucky dip barrel contains 40 identical boxes. 4 of these contain a large prize and 8 contain smaller prizes. Find the probability that a box picked at random contains:

a a large prize   **b** any prize   **c** no prize.

5 The probability that a train arrives early is 0.2 and the probability that it arrives on time is 0.5. Find the probability that the train arrives:

a early or on time   **b** late

6 A card game has 30 cards with a picture and information about a different wild animal on each. 12 of them show mammals, 9 show birds, 5 show amphibians and 4 show sharks.

If a card is picked at random, find the probability that the animal:

a is a mammal   **b** is a bird or an amphibian

c is not a bird   **d** can live in the water.

7 A box of milk chocolates contains 8 with toffee centres, 6 with nuts, 5 with fruit-flavoured centres and 6 which are solid chocolate.

Find the probability that a chocolate picked at random is:

a fruit flavoured   **b** not solid chocolate

c nut or toffee centred   **d** a dark chocolate.

Write your answers as decimal fractions.

8 In a game Callum uses a 20-sided dice that has the numbers 1 to 20 on its sides. Find the probability that the number he rolls is:

a a 7   **b** an even number   **c** a prime number

d a number with a 2 in it   **e** a 6 or a multiple of 4   **f** not a factor of 20.

9 Two classes from S1 and S2 carried out a survey to find out what colours of eyes they had. The results are recorded in the table.

Eye colour	S1		S2	
	Girls	Boys	Girls	Boys
Blue	2	4	2	1
Green	2	2	3	5
Brown	7	3	3	2
Other	0	0	1	3

Find the probability that a pupil picked at random:

a has blue eyes   **b** is an S2 pupil with green eyes

c is an S1 girl with brown eyes   **d** is not in S1

e is an S2 boy with blue or brown eyes.

10 A charity is holding a raffle to raise funds. They sell 200 tickets, 50 of which are green, 50 are white, 50 are pink and 50 are blue. The tickets in each colour are numbered from 1 to 50. A ticket wins a prize if its number ends in either 0 or 5.

Find the probability that a ticket:

a wins a prize   **b** is pink   **c** is a green winning ticket   **d** is not blue.

Write your answers as decimal fractions.

Exercise 31B Listing outcomes and making choices

1   **a** Use a two-way table to list all the possible outcomes from rolling two dice and adding their scores.

b Use your table to find the probability that the total is:

     i 5   **ii** greater than 9   **iii** a double

     iv 6 or 7   **v** a multiple of 2.

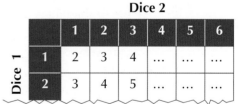

c Use your table to decide if this statement is true:

'Each dice is equally likely to roll a number from 1 to 6, so all totals from 1 to 12 have the same chance of happening'.

Explain your answer.

2 The local sandwich shop offers five types of filling: egg salad, tuna mayonnaise, BLT, cheese and pickle, and ham and mustard. You can also choose to have white, brown or granary bread.

List all the possible combinations of filling and bread. How many different choices are there?

3 Mark has a collection of shirts and ties to wear to work. His ties are blue, red or multi-coloured and his shirts are either white or blue.

a If he picks them at random each day, what are all the possible combinations of shirts and ties?

b Find the probability that he picks:

i a blue shirt and a blue tie

ii a white shirt and a red tie

iii a blue shirt and either a red or a multi-coloured tie.

4 **a** Use a two-way table to list all the possible outcomes of tossing a coin and rolling a dice.

b Use your list to find the probability of throwing:

i a tail and a 4   **ii** a head and a number greater than 4

iii a tail and an even number   **iv** any result without a 6 in it.

5 Gemma has these two five-sided spinners and spins both together.

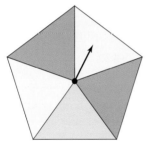 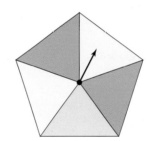

a List all the possible outcomes.

b Find the probability that:

i both spinners show red

ii one spinner shows red and the other spinner shows yellow

iii neither spinner shows red

iv the spinners show different colours.

6 Use the probabilities of each of these events to decide which option to pick.

a The weather forecast says the probability of rain is 25%. Should you take your jacket with you or leave it at home?

b You have to pay £1 to play a dice game. You win £2 if you roll a 6, but lose if you roll any other number. Would you play the game?

c In a card game, you need to predict if the next card will be higher or lower to win the game. The probability of the next card being higher is $\frac{7}{13}$

Should you pick higher or lower?

7 Julie has two sisters, so she tells her friends that her mum's new baby will definitely be a boy. Is she correct?

8 In a board game, Alice needs to roll a 6 on a fair dice to start moving round the board. She still hasn't rolled it after 10 attempts, so complains that it is harder to roll a 6 than any other number. Explain why she is wrong.

9 A game involves tossing two coins and you win if both are heads. There are four outcomes: HH, HT, TH and TT. Trevor says that this means that you are certain to win if you play four times, but Tina disagrees and says it could take a lot more attempts to win. Who is correct?

10 Ben's class are playing a probability game where you score the value shown on a 1–6 dice, but get knocked out if a 1 is rolled. The first five rolls were 6, 5, 4, 3 and 2, so Ben thinks that the next score is bound to be a 1. Is he correct?

Exercise 31C Expectation

1 The probability of winning a prize in a charity raffle is 0.2.

How many prizes would you expect to win if you bought 20 tickets?

> **Hint** Expected number of successes = probability of success × number of trials

2 The probability of getting rain in November is $\frac{3}{5}$

How many days of rain would you expect during the month?

3 If you cut a well-shuffled, full deck of cards, the probability of picking a heart is 0.25.

How many times would you expect to get a heart if you cut the deck 12 times?

4 The probability of the bus you take to and from school each day being late is 0.2.

How many times would you expect it to be late over a 2-week period?

5 There are 200 coloured sweets in a bag. If 15 of them are blue:

a find the probability of picking a blue sweet

b how many blue sweets would you expect to get if you randomly picked 40 sweets?

6 A game involves tossing two coins and you win if both are tails.

a Find the probability of getting two tails.

b How many times would you expect to win if you play 12 times?

7 There are 330 pupils in S1, of whom 44 are left handed. If you randomly picked 30 pupils to take part in a focus group, how many would you expect to be left handed?

8 In a dice game, you score the total of rolling two dice. If there are 72 rolls in a game, how many times would you expect to get a score of 9?